Charmaine Solomon's THAI Cookbook

CHARLES E. TUTTLE COMPANY
Boston • Rutland, Vermont • Tokyo

First United States publication 1991
First paperback edition 1994

Published by Charles E. Tuttle Co., Inc
153 Milk Street
Boston, Massachusetts 02109

ISBN 0-8048-3039-8
Cataloging -in-Publication data for this book is available from the Library of Congress.

Produced in conjunction with Coral Press by Penguin Books Australia
487 Maroondah Highway, PO Box 257
Ringwood, Victoria 3134, Australia

Typeset in Australia by Solo Typesetting
Printed in Singapore by Kyodo Printing Co. Pte Ltd

Managing Editor: David McGonigal
Recipe Editor: Dawn Hope
Design by Ken Gilroy
Food styling by Jill Pavey, Charmaine Solomon and Darlene Macklyn
Photography by Ray Joyce
Photographs of Thailand by Robbi Newman and David McGonigal
Cover design by Cathy Larsen

Acknowledgements
The author would like to thank Thai International Airways and the Tourist
Authority of Thailand for their help during the research for this book. Thanks
must also go to the many cooks of Thailand who contributed recipes and gave
unstintingly of their time. The assistance of Royal Doulton Australia and
Wedgwood Australia in supplying chinaware for photographing the dishes is also
gratefully acknowleged.

Contents

Introduction

As in most great cuisines there is, in Thailand, a classic cuisine and a peasant cuisine. Both are full of intriguing flavours. While everyday meals are down-to-earth, classic Thai cuisine is reminiscent of French *haute cuisine* of years gone by – elaborate table arrangements, exquisitely detailed garnishes, the perfuming of food with herbs and even flowers. There is more romance in Thai cooking than any other cuisine in the world today.

While writing my *Complete Asian Cookbook*, which took in the cuisines of 15 countries and has become a standard work on the subject, the chapter on Thailand was one of the most fascinating to research and cook my way through, so I have particularly enjoyed delving deeply into the cuisine for this book.

The flavours were familiar to me because they have much in common with the food of Burma, with which Thailand shares a border. This is where my mother's family lived, where I visited during my formative years, and (like most people) I have a nostalgic fondness for foods remembered from childhood. But there is an added dimension to Thai food which enthuses and inspires me as I discover more about it. I suppose one can only describe it as sophistication and refinement . . . especially in regard to what is known as 'palace cuisine'.

There is an unmistakable spectrum of flavours embodying the heart and soul of Thai food. It is not mere prettiness which captures the imagination. Even peasant cuisine is both subtle and pungent, a glorious awakening of the tastebuds that makes you wonder, on tasting Thai food for the first time, why you have never experienced this before.

Now the world is waking up to the flavours of Thailand. I have tasted the real thing as far afield as Denmark and England. Australia has gone wild over Thai cuisine. It is alive and flourishing in the United States and its refinement and fresh flavours are regarded with admiration in other Asian countries.

Thai food is totally individual, befitting a country which has never been conquered, yet it has similarities to both Indian and Chinese food. From the former comes the use of fragrant spices in certain dishes. The Chinese influence shows in the use of noodles made from rice, wheat and bean starch. Their curved cooking pans, *ka-tha*, are just like the familiar wok, but often made in brass rather than steel. Because of the curved shape, very little oil is necessary, but ingredients must be kept constantly on the move and therefore the technique of stir-frying is as popular in Thai cooking as in Chinese cooking. Of course, you can use a frying pan but because it has a large, flat cooking surface it will be necessary to increase the amount of oil used.

Where soy sauce is indispensable in Chinese food, in Thai cooking it is replaced by fish sauce – *nam pla*. Thin, salty, not terribly fishy in spite of its name, it brings out other flavours and is universally added to each and every dish. If a more pronounced fish flavour is required, it is obtained from *kapi*, a paste made from shrimps, similar to the *blachan* of Malaysia and the *ngapi* of Burma.

Rice is the cornerstone of Thai cuisine. Every meal is built around a large amount of freshly-cooked white rice. The best Thai rice is jasmine rice – white, long-grained, with a faint and delightful perfume. It is cooked without adding salt since the food that accompanies the rice is highly seasoned and salty. The rice is brought to the table in a covered bowl or individual woven baskets so it is kept steaming hot throughout the meal. In true Thai fashion, all the food is brought to the table at once and will include *khao* (rice), *kaeng* (dishes with gravy), *krueng kieng* (side dishes) and *kaeng chud* (soup).

In elegant Thai restaurants the meal is served in stages, much in the manner of a Western meal. First, two or more small appetisers with dipping sauces. Then the main course of rice accompanied by soup, curry, a fried dish, a steamed dish, a salad. When cooking at home and you wish to extend a meal to serve more people, make an extra dish or two and increase the amount of rice.

While desserts are not a feature of a Thai meal, invariably one cannot resist ordering some of the attractive sweets which are offered on every menu.

Order a plate of fruit in a Thai hotel and it will be brought to you with every fruit shaped like some rare, exotic flower. Small round watermelons are transformed into dahlias or lotus blossoms, each petal curled as in nature, edged with white and blushing deep pink towards the centre as the knife cuts

deeper. The red pawpaws look like tulips, even dull brown sapodillas are made to look as good as they taste.

Have a meal at a good restaurant and notice the vegetable garnishes – carrots emerge as marigolds, or as ears of golden wheat. Turnips and radishes become roses, cucumbers turn into water lilies, gourds become carved receptacles for dipping sauces. Watching a demonstration, I am amazed at the speed, dexterity and precision with which this carving is done, even by girls not yet in their teens.

While this may be for admiring rather than copying, I would like to assure the enthusiastic amateur.that it is quite possible for someone who isn't born to this art to acquire it. My friend and fellow-cook, Jill Pavey, Australian to her fingertips, was mainly responsible for the carvings of leaves and flowers which garnish the dishes throughout this book. I have carved the odd radish or chilli, but it is Jill who, by dint of much practice, can turn out a cucumber leaf in 30 seconds flat! With our willing husbands we travelled through Thailand together, tasting, learning and recording recipes.

If you get the impression I'm somewhat partial to Thai food and cooking, you're perfectly correct – it forms a considerable part of the meals I cook for my family. However, all the enthusiasm in the world doesn't ensure your busy schedule will allow you to start 'from scratch' each time. So I've arrived at ways to take the fuss and fiddle out of presenting a Thai meal. After all, there's no rule against making things easy.

If you shop for ingredients each time you want to cook Thai, chances are you'll do it far less frequently than you would like to. But if you convert those fresh ingredients into long-lasting supplies of curry pastes and store them in the refrigerator or freezer, preparation time is cut dramatically. Be assured, no authenticity is lost using this system . . . much as I enjoy cooking, there are other demands on my time and, I know, on yours too.

I wish you as much enjoyment in using this book as I have had in researching it, testing the recipes, and trying to make it simple and rewarding to cook authentic, delicious Thai food in your own kitchen.

Coconut Milk, and Other

Coconut milk is one of the essentials of Thai cooking, used in everything from soup to dessert. There are ways to make it if you cannot purchase the canned or instant product, and I'll explain these in some detail.

Curry pastes, too, are basic in Thai cooking. Since they appear in many recipes, here they are given a section of their own, with suggestions on how to greatly cut down the time involved by making larger quantities than you need for a single dish. If you're really into Thai food and cook it often, this is a great time saver. Refrigerate curry paste in screw-top jars for up to four weeks and use as required. Or freeze the paste in meal-sized amounts to have ready whenever you have a yen for those incomparable flavours.

Coconut milk and cream

Thankfully, there are not many writers now who refer to the clear liquid inside a coconut as 'coconut milk'. This was a common misconception among Western food writers even as recently as a decade ago, but since Asian food has become popular worldwide, people are better educated about ingredients and generally know that coconut milk is the rich white liquid extracted from the *flesh* of mature coconuts.

If you can purchase good quality

unsweetened coconut milk in cans, do so. Many suburban supermarkets now stock coconut milk and there are several excellent brands.

Where *coconut cream* or *thick coconut milk* is called for, use it straight from the can without diluting. For *coconut milk*, mix equal parts of canned coconut milk and water. If the ingredient is termed *thin coconut milk*, dilute one part canned coconut milk with two parts water.

For curries and other savoury dishes, I would not hesitate to use either canned coconut milk or instant dried coconut milk powder. Try various brands and choose one that contains no sugar, is white rather than grey in appearance, and smooth rather than clotted. Coconut milk is very perishable and if not using any remaining milk the same day, freeze it in ice-cube trays. When they are solid, pop them into a freezer bag – a handy way to add a tablespoon or two of coconut milk to enrich a soup or sauce.

Reconstitute instant dried coconut milk powder according to the directions on the label. Taste, and if necessary use more powder to give a richer result. The convenience of this is that you make only as much as you need each time.

If canned or instant coconut milk powder is not readily available where you shop, you can prepare it by using either fresh coconut or

Curry Pastes
Basic Flavours

desiccated coconut.

While thankful for the convenience of these products, it must be said that in certain desserts you do need the incomparable flavour of fresh coconut milk which has not been treated by the extreme heat needed to sterilise canned and dried products. For such recipes, it is essential to know how to make fresh coconut milk.

First choose your coconut. It should be full of water, devoid of any dampness on the shell, and there should be no mould, or moisture leaking through any of the three spots at one end. When opened, it should smell sweet and fresh.

To open a coconut, the best way is to heft it in one hand and, wielding a hammer or the back of a cleaver with the other hand, tap firmly around the middle of the nut. When a deep crack appears, insert the corner of the cleaver blade and let the water run into a jug. (If the nut is very fresh, the water makes a nice drink.) A few more blows and it will break in two. If possible, grate the white portion right in the shell with a grater made expressly for coconut (*see* Implements, *page 24*). It is a thankless task prising the flesh from the shell and using the usual straight-sided grater . . . skinned knuckles at the very least are what you get for your trouble!

Pour 2 cups (16 fl oz) hot water over the grated flesh of one coconut and knead hard, then strain through a fine sieve, pressing out as much moisture as possible. This is the first extract, or *thick milk*. Pour more water over the grated coconut and knead again to extract more milk. Strain. This is *thin milk*. Repeat once more. Unless thick coconut milk is specified, use a combination of thick and thin milk in most recipes.

If a recipe calls for *coconut cream*, use the rich layer that forms on top of the first extract after it has been left in the refrigerator for an hour or so.

If fresh coconuts are not available, use desiccated coconut or shredded unsweetened coconut. Put 2 cups (6 oz) desiccated coconut in a bowl and pour 2½ cups (20 fl oz) hot water over it. Allow to cool to lukewarm. Knead firmly for a few minutes and strain through a fine strainer or muslin, pressing out as much liquid as possible. This should yield about 1½ cups (12 fl oz) *thick coconut milk*.

Repeat the process, using the same coconut and another 2½ cups hot water. Because of the moisture retained in the coconut, it should yield about 2 cups (16 fl oz) of *thin coconut milk*.

A blender or food processor makes this procedure quicker and easier, taking the place of kneading, but straining and pressing out the liquid still must be done.

For a richer coconut milk, use hot milk instead of hot water.

Fresh ginger root

Fresh hot chillies

Dried chillies

Lemon grass

Halved lime
and whole kaffir lime

Kaffir lime leaves:
fresh, frozen
and dried

Garlic
chives

Pandanus
leaves

Fresh coriander

Fresh mint

Small and large leaf basil of various types

Spring onions

Large purple onions

Garlic: fresh bulb
and dried flakes

Small purple
shallots

Ground, dried turmeric,
and fresh turmeric

You are looking
at the soul of
Thai cooking -
the fragrant
herbs and
pungent spices
which make it
taste like no
other cuisine
on earth.

Dried
tamarind pulp

Galangal: fresh root, frozen and dried slices

Black and green
pepper corns

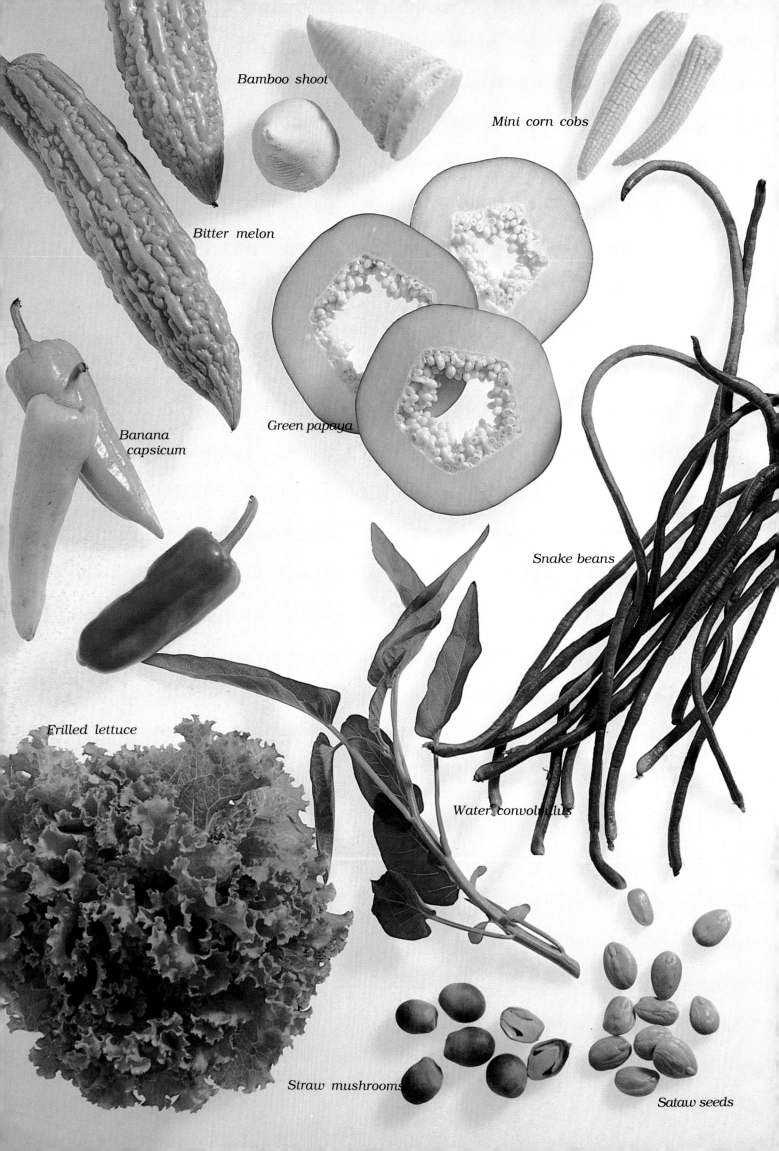

Bamboo shoot

Mini corn cobs

Bitter melon

Banana capsicum

Green papaya

Snake beans

Frilled lettuce

Water convolvulus

Straw mushrooms

Sataw seeds

Giant white radish

Water chestnuts

Snow peas

Besides the everyday vegetables, there are some which are native to South-East Asia and are now becoming better known abroad.

Slender white eggplant (aubergine)

Slender purple eggplant (aubergine)

Dried mushrooms

Fresh coconut

Small round purple and white eggplants (aubergines)

Small round green eggplants

Fresh bean shoots

Tiny, pea-sized eggplant (aubergines)

Cummin seed

Kaffir lime leaves

Dried shrimp paste

Dried red chillies

Chilli powder

Dried galangal

Fresh lemon grass

Black pepper

Coriander seed

Grated lime rind

Fresh coriander

Garlic

Coriander roots

ll brown onions

Red curry paste

und turmeric

Green curry paste

Green chillies

Curry pastes

It is possible to purchase ready-made curry pastes, and most of these are very good, but some are inclined to be harsh and the ingredients include monosodium glutamate, which many people prefer to do without.

I have yet to find a green curry paste on the shelf as good and fresh tasting as one made from the recipe given on page 21. For those dedicated cooks who prefer to make their own spice and herb blends, I have set out the formulas I use, preceded by recommendations on handling certain ingredients. Please note them carefully; they have been learned by sometimes painful trial and error!

Chillies (*Prik*):

Handling chillies can be a searing experience, so wear gloves or take care not to handle the cut surfaces. If you do handle cut chillies, as soon as you finish wash your hands in cold water, rubbing your fingers well with bicarbonate of soda (baking soda). It soothes the burning sensation. I find that holding the chilli by its stem and taking care to avoid the volatile oils is well worth the trouble. PLEASE don't touch your eyes with hands which have recently touched chillies, and be mindful of touching children.

If you like a hot curry, leave in the seeds but if you prefer less heat, remove them. Slit fresh chillies and flip out the seeds with the point of a knife. Snip off stems of dried chillies and shake out the seeds, snip or break the chillies in pieces and soak in hot water for 15 minutes to soften.

Coriander (*Pak chee*):

Peculiar to Thai cooking is the use of the roots of the coriander (cilantro/Chinese parsley) plant. Many shops sell the plant without the roots, which is all right for Indian or Chinese food but lacks the vital part for Thai cooking. Wash the plants thoroughly, scrubbing the roots clean. Separate the lower part of the stems under a cold tap so any sand is flushed away. Since bunches of coriander can be large or small and even individual plants can vary greatly in size, to give some uniformity I have measured it, roughly chopped, in cup or spoon measures.

Kaffir lime leaves and rind (*Makrut*):

Look for shops specialising in Thai ingredients and buy fresh or frozen lime leaves for the best flavour. If you cannot find these, use the dried leaves, first soaking them in boiling water for 20–30 minutes. Or use fresh lime or lemon leaves if you have them growing, although they are not as fragrant as kaffir lime. There are two sections to a kaffir lime leaf so, when counting them out, if they are broken allow two pieces for each leaf required.

The rind of kaffir limes is also used for intense citrus flavour and the best way to obtain this (unless you have access to fresh limes) is to buy frozen kaffir limes. Keep them in the freezer so they are very hard, then grate on the fine surface of a grater. Use only the coloured portion, not the white pith underneath. The rind is also sold dried, but because it has the white pith with it, I find it rather bitter. Use it if you like, but in small quantities. A suitable alternative is the rind of fresh Tahitian or West Indian limes.

10 fresh or dried hot red chillies
½ cup small purple shallots or 2 small brown onions, chopped
1 tablespoon chopped garlic
¼ cup finely sliced lemon grass, or the thinly peeled rind of 1 lemon
1 tablespoon chopped galangal, fresh or frozen, or 3 teaspoons powdered galangal
1 tablespoon chopped fresh coriander (cilantro/Chinese parsley) roots
1 tablespoon chopped fresh coriander stems
1 teaspoon finely grated kaffir lime rind
4 kaffir lime leaves, mid-ribs removed
2 tablespoons oil
2 teaspoons dried shrimp paste
1 tablespoon coriander seeds
2 teaspoons cummin seeds
1 teaspoon black peppercorns
2 teaspoons paprika
1 teaspoon ground turmeric

Red curry paste
(*Kruang Kaeng Dang*)

Makes about 1 cup (8 fl oz)

In the container of an electric blender put the chillies, shallots, garlic, lemon grass, galangal, coriander roots and stems, lime rind and the lime leaves. Add the oil and blend to a smooth purée.

Wrap the shrimp paste closely in foil, flattening to make a small packet. Place under a hot griller (broiler) and cook 2 or 3 minutes on each side.

In a small saucepan toast the coriander seeds until golden and fragrant, then turn onto a plate. Toast the cummin seeds until fragrant. Lightly toast the peppercorns also, and grind all three to a powder in a mortar and pestle. Add to the blender with the paprika and ground turmeric and shrimp paste. Blend once more.

Store in a clean, dry bottle in the refrigerator for 3–4 weeks, or divide into convenient portions, wrap and freeze.

Green curry paste
(Kruang Kaeng Khiew Wan)

4 large or 8 small green chillies

½ cup purple shallots or 1 medium onion, chopped

1 tablespoon chopped garlic

½ cup chopped fresh coriander (cilantro/Chinese parsley), including roots, stems and leaves

¼ cup finely sliced lemon grass, or the thinly peeled rind of 1 lemon

1 tablespoon chopped galangal, fresh or frozen

2 teaspoons ground coriander

1 teaspoon ground cummin

1 teaspoon black peppercorns

1 teaspoon ground turmeric

1 teaspoon dried shrimp paste

2 tablespoons oil

Don't let the colour fool you, a green curry can be devastatingly hot if prepared the traditional way. For less heat, discard the chilli seeds.
Makes about 1 cup (8 fl oz)

Remove the stems and roughly chop the chillies. Put into an electric blender with all the other ingredients and blend to a smooth paste. Add a tablespoon of extra oil or a little water if necessary to facilitate blending.

Store as for Red Curry Paste.

Masaman (Muslim) curry paste
(Kruang Kaeng Masaman)

7–10 dried red chillies, or 2 teaspoons chilli powder

2 tablespoons oil

2 medium onions, chopped

1 tablespoon chopped garlic

1 teaspoon dried shrimp paste

2 teaspoons finely chopped lemon grass, or lemon rind

1 tablespoon chopped galangal, or 2 teaspoons powdered galangal

2 tablespoons coriander seeds or ground coriander

2 teaspoons cummin seeds, or ground cummin

1 teaspoon fennel seeds, or ground fennel

1 teaspoon ground cinnamon

½ teaspoon ground cardamom

½ teaspoon ground nutmeg or mace

¼ teaspoon ground cloves

Influenced by the Muslims from India, as evidenced by the use of fragrant spices.
Makes about ¾ cup (6 fl oz)

Break the chillies, shake out the seeds and soak the chillies in boiling water for 10–15 minutes.

Heat the oil and fry the onions and garlic over low heat until they are soft and start turning brown. Add the shrimp paste and fry for a minute longer, crushing it in the oil with the back of a spoon. Remove from heat and when cool put it into the container of an electric blender with the soaked and drained chillies, lemon grass and galangal. Blend to a smooth purée, adding a little water if necessary to facilitate blending.

In a dry pan roast the coriander seeds until brown, shaking the pan or stirring frequently. Turn out and allow to cool while roasting the cummin and fennel seeds slightly. Pound all the seeds in a mortar and pestle to a fine powder. If using ground coriander, cummin and fennel, they may be combined and dry-roasted in a small pan, using low heat and stirring constantly to ensure they do not burn. Roast until they are a rich brown colour and have a fine aromatic smell. Combine with the puréed ingredients, and add the ground cinnamon, cardamom, nutmeg and cloves. Bottle and store in the refrigerator.

½ cup (4 fl oz) vegetable oil

2 teaspoons chilli powder

1 tablespoon water

½ cup dried shrimp

½ cup finely sliced lemon grass

1 tablespoon finely chopped garlic

2 tablespoons chopped coriander (cilantro/Chinese parsley) roots

10 whole peppercorns

1 tablespoon galangal, finely chopped, or 2 teaspoons dried galangal powder

4 fresh red chillies

4 fresh green chillies

8 fresh, frozen or dried kaffir lime leaves (soaked if they are dried)

4 tablespoons (3 fl oz) fish sauce

4 tablespoons (3 fl oz) lime juice

1 teaspoon ground turmeric

1 tablespoon dried shrimp paste

1 tablespoon salt

1 tablespoon sugar

1 tablespoon citric acid

1 teaspoon finely grated lime rind

Hot and sour soup paste (*Tom yum* paste)

Although basically a flavouring for the tongue-tingling *tom yum* soups made with prawns, chicken or other main ingredients, this is a wonderful flavouring for other dishes too. I feel lost without a constant supply of it in the refrigerator.
Makes about 1½ cups (12 fl oz)

Pour the oil into a warm wok or frying pan and on low heat cook the chilli powder mixed with the water, stirring, until the oil turns red. In an electric blender reduce the dried shrimp to a floss and empty into a bowl.

Put the lemon grass, garlic, coriander, peppercorns, galangal, fresh chillies and kaffir lime leaves into the electric blender with the fish sauce and lime juice, and blend at high speed to a smooth purée. Add to the wok together with the turmeric, shrimp paste and shrimp floss and cook, stirring frequently, until the oil comes to the surface. Cool, stir in the salt, sugar, citric acid and lime rind. Store in a clean, dry glass bottle, tightly covered, in the refrigerator for 3–4 weeks; or freeze in 1 or 2 tablespoon amounts for longer periods.

Note: To make a soup for 4 people, use 1–2 tablespoons of this paste, 250 g (8 oz) chicken or prawns (shrimp) and 3 cups (24 fl oz) stock. Add extra fresh lime juice to accentuate the refreshingly sour flavour.

Coconut Milk, Curry Pastes and Other Basic Flavours

10 long dried chillies
½ cup (4 fl oz) hot water
1 teaspoon grated kaffir lime rind
4 slices galangal, fresh, frozen or dried
½ cup chopped shallots, or spring onions (scallions)
2 stalks lemon grass, finely sliced
1 tablespoon chopped garlic
8 fresh coriander (cilantro/Chinese parsley) roots, chopped
1 tablespoon whole black peppercorns
2 teaspoons shrimp paste
1 tablespoon fish sauce
2 teaspoons salt
½ cup (4 oz) crunchy peanut butter
⅓ cup (2½ fl oz) peanut oil

Panang curry paste
(Kruang Kaeng Panang)

Makes about 1½ cups

Break open the chillies, discard the stems and seeds, and soak the chillies in hot water for 15 minutes. Put the chillies with the soaking water and all the remaining ingredients, except the peanut butter and oil, into an electric blender and blend to a smooth purée.

Stir in the peanut butter and oil, bottle and store in the refrigerator. Use about 3 tablespoons of this curry paste to each 500 g (1 lb) meat or poultry.

1 tablespoon chopped garlic
2 teaspoons salt
2 tablespoons whole black peppercorns
2 cups well-washed, coarsely chopped fresh coriander (cilantro/Chinese parsley), including roots
2 tablespoons lemon juice

Pepper and coriander paste
(Rark Pak Chee, Prik Thai)

These are such basic flavourings for Thai food that I find this recipe saves a great deal of the time spent making the mixture each time it is needed. It takes almost as long to make a small quantity as a large one, so store some in the refrigerator ready for your adventures in Thai cooking. So far I have not come across this mixture bottled commercially.

Makes about 1 cup (8 fl oz)

Crush the garlic with the salt to a smooth paste. Roast the peppercorns in a dry pan for a minute or two, then coarsely crush in a mortar and pestle. Finely chop the coriander roots, leaves and stems. Mix all together, adding the lemon juice.

This paste may also be made in a blender, but in this case reduce the black peppercorns to 1 tablespoon because it is hotter if finely ground than if coarsely crushed.

Implements

I assure you that it is possible to cook Thai food with just a few basic saucepans, a frying pan, an ordinary wooden spoon, and a colander. So please don't look at the utensils in the picture and think "Heavens, I don't have any of those. I won't be able to cope with the recipes in this book."

The photograph shows what I use at home and it's included because they do make some tasks easier, and that is what this book is all about — delicious Thai food with no hassles. Of course, you can improvise a steamer with a large boiler, in which you place a trivet then balance a cake rack on it. And you don't have to use a wok: a frying pan will do the job; just be aware that it will require more oil than is called for in a wok, and it won't be as easy to stir-fry as it is in a rounded utensil.

In some cases, I pass over the authentic article in everyday use. For example, my electric blender does the job faster than a mortar and pestle and with less effort on my part. But sometimes I do pound away because there is only a small amount to be ground and the blender needs a fair quantity to work effectively.

However, in other cases the utensil shown is the only one that will do a decent job so you need to know about it. Coconut graters are a good case in point. Notice the shape of both the old-fashioned brass grater and the modern plastic one. They fit into the coconut shell and do away with the necessity for dangerous procedures (*see page 13*). The little fluted mould on a wooden handle (for Golden Cups, *page 45*) is an improvisation of my own — a French tartlet tin wired to a handle after drilling a tiny hole in the top edge of the tin and the bottom of the handle.

If you have a chance to browse in Asian shops look for items which will be most useful to you and make it easy to cook the beautiful food of Thailand.

1   Tiered aluminium steamer
2   Black enamel wok
3   Brass pan, ladle, wok chan
4   Bamboo steaming baskets
5   Clay cooking pots
6   Clay mortar and wooden pestle
7   Wire mesh basket on long
     bamboo handle for boiling
8   Wire mesh frying spoon
9   Woven baskets for serving rice
10 Electric blender and small blender jar
11 Choppers
12 Small pointed knives
13 Corrugated cutters for sweets
14 Coconut graters
15 Krathong mould

Appetisers and

In Thai cuisine, appetisers and savouries are very important. People love the small savoury bites which are sold on the streets, served at parties, or before a meal. While there are no 'courses' as there are in a Western meal, these could easily be described as *hors d'oeuvres*, meaning 'outside the menu'. Some are fairly substantial, two- or three-bite sized, but most are very dainty; all are readily classified as finger food. In Thailand, when catering for those who eat on the run, extra seasonings may frequently be in powdered form – sugar, salt, crushed roasted peanuts or sesame seeds. But when eating at a

Savoury Snacks

table, as people do at the food stalls at all hours of the day and night, many savoury snacks come with their own dipping sauces.

The range of Thai appetisers and savoury snacks is fascinating. Some are wrapped in edible leaves, others in leaves which flavour the food but are then discarded. Some are savoury mixtures folded in paper-thin, transparent dough. Others are served in hollowed-out fruit or water chestnuts. Everything is so pretty. Morsels that will vanish in a single mouthful are still presented with incredibly detailed decoration.

Filling:

250 g (8 oz) white fish fillets

½ teaspoon crushed garlic

1 teaspoon finely grated fresh ginger

¼ teaspoon salt

⅛ teaspoon ground black pepper

1 teaspoon finely chopped coriander (cilantro/Chinese parsley) roots

1 teaspoon finely chopped kaffir lime rind

2 teaspoons fish sauce

2 tablespoons finely chopped spring onions (scallions)

Dough:

1 cup (4 oz) gluten-free flour (e.g. wheat starch)

3 tablespoons maize cornflour (cornstarch)

¾ cup (6 fl oz) boiling water

1 tablespoon oil

¼ teaspoon salt

Steamed fish dumplings
(Khanom Jeeb Pla)

Encased in a semi-transparent dough and steamed, the fish filling in these small dumplings is tasty but not hot. One of the intriguing characteristics of Thai food is that so many things seems to be in miniature.
Makes about 20

Filling:
Remove any traces of skin and bones from the fish and cut into pieces. Put through a food processor or chop very finely. Add all the other filling ingredients and mix well. Cover and refrigerate while preparing the dough.

Dough:
Sift the flours into a bowl. In a small saucepan bring the water to the boil. Add the oil and salt and pour onto the flour, stirring constantly with a wooden spoon. When cool enough to handle, knead lightly until smooth. Divide into two equal portions and shape each into a cyclinder about 2.5 cm (1 in) in diameter. Wrap in plastic film to prevent the surface drying out.

Cut in 1 cm (½ in) slices and roll out one slice at a time, until thin and about 10 cm (4 in) in diameter. Neaten the edges by cutting with a scone (biscuit) cutter. Place a teaspoonful of the filling on the dough, fold over and press the edges together to seal. Make a decorative rope edge as shown in the step-by-step photographs.

Place the dumplings on lightly oiled squares of greaseproof or non-stick baking paper in a steamer (or on a cake cooler placed on a trivet in a large pan). Cover the pan and steam over boiling water for 8–10 minutes. Serve warm, with a dipping sauce.

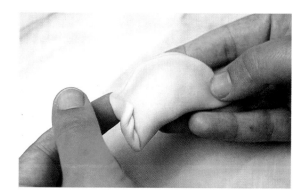

Filling:

1 tablespoon oil	
2 teaspoons finely chopped coriander (cilantro/Chinese parsley) roots	
2 teaspoons finely chopped garlic	
500 g (1 lb) minced (ground) beef or pork	
3 tablespoons fish sauce	
¼ teaspoon ground black pepper	
1 teaspoon ground turmeric	
1 teaspoon ground cummin	
2 teaspoons ground coriander	
1 hot chilli, finely chopped (optional)	
½ cup raw potato, cut into tiny (6 mm/¼ in) dice	
2 teaspoons sugar	

Pastry:

2 cups (8 oz) plain (all-purpose) flour
½ teaspoon salt
60 g (2 oz) butter
¼ cup (2 fl oz) coconut milk
oil for deep-frying

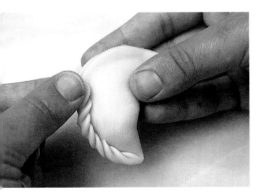

Deep-fried curry puffs
(Kari Puff)

The weekend market in Bangkok is an experience no visitor to Thailand should miss. There they were selling curry puffs so tiny that I wondered at the fact that each still had a perfect rope edge decoration. One small mouthful, nothing more. We tried making them this size. It is possible, but there's no denying that it's easier when they are just a little larger, like those pictured.
Makes about 20

Filling:
Heat the oil in a wok or frying pan and cook the coriander roots and garlic over gentle heat until golden. Add the beef or pork, raise heat to medium-high and stir-fry until it changes colour. Add the fish sauce, pepper, turmeric, cummin and coriander, and stir well. Cover and cook on low heat for 25 minutes, or until the meat is tender and the liquid is reduced.

Stir in the chilli, potatoes and sugar, cover and cook for 10 minutes longer. The potatoes should be firm. If necessary, cook uncovered for the final few minutes so the liquid evaporates completely. Remove from heat and allow to cool.

Pastry:
Sift the flour and salt, rub in the butter and add sufficient coconut milk to make a fairly firm dough. Form into a ball and knead lightly on a floured board until smooth. Wrap in plastic film and chill for at least 30 minutes.

On a floured surface roll out the pastry to about 3 mm (⅛ in) thickness. Cut into 10 cm (4 in) circles and brush the edges with cold water . Place a tablespoon of the cooled filling on each circle slightly below the centre. Bring the pastry over the filling and press the edges together to seal.

To make the rope edge, fold over one corner of the pastry at a 45 degree angle and press it flat. Then fold over the next section to make a rough triangle over the first fold. Repeat around the edge of the pastry, pressing each fold as you go.

Heat oil for deep-frying and fry a few puffs at a time until golden brown. The oil should be hot enough to cook them in a couple of minutes. If it is not hot enough, the pastry will be heavy and oily instead of crisp and light. Drain on absorbent paper and serve warm or at room temperature.

To make ahead:
This is an ideal recipe to make ahead and freeze, leaving only the final frying to be done. When the curry puffs are made, arrange them on a baking tray (not touching) and freeze until firm. Then pack into freezer bags, extract the air and return to freezer. They will keep for 2 months without loss of quality. To thaw, arrange them on a tray lined with absorbent paper and cover with more paper so the melting ice crystals are absorbed.

12 x 15 cm (6 in) diameter circles of double foil or banana leaf
500 g (1 lb) white fish fillets
1½ cup (12 fl oz) thick coconut milk
2 tablespoons Red Curry Paste (*page 20*)
2 eggs, lightly beaten
1 tablespoon fish sauce
1 teaspoon salt
1 teaspoon finely chopped *Krachai* (*see page 209*) (optional)
1 teaspoon shrimp paste
1 cup basil leaves, tightly packed
3 teaspoons rice flour
1 or 2 kaffir lime leaves, very finely shredded
2 red chillies, finely sliced
12 fresh coriander (cilantro/ Chinese parsley) leaves

Steamed fish pudding

(Hor Mok Pla)

This steamed fish pudding may be cooked in one large dish instead of the individual cups pictured, in which case it will need 25–30 minutes cooking time.
Serves 6

Make the cups to hold the fish puddings. Make 4 folds evenly spaced as shown in the step by step photographs, and fasten with staples or toothpicks.

Clean the fish very carefully so it is free of all bones and skin. Process the fish to a purée in a food processor or chop it finely. Mix ¾ cup (6 fl oz) of the coconut milk with the red curry paste and knead well with the fish. Stir in the beaten eggs, fish sauce, salt, *krachai* and shrimp paste, combining thoroughly.

Divide the basil leaves between the cups, then put about 2 or 3 tablespoons of the fish mixture in each. Tap each cup gently on the kitchen bench to settle the contents. Place the cups on a rack in a steamer and steam over boiling water for 10–12 minutes.

Combine the remaining ¾ cup of coconut milk. Move the steamer away from the heat and put 2 teaspoons of the coconut milk and rice flour mixture in each cup. Scatter a few shreds of lime leaf and chilli slices on top, return to heat and steam for a further 2 or 3 minutes. Garnish each with a coriander leaf before serving.

Steamed fish cups

2 eggs

1 tablespoon water

¼ teaspoon salt

2 tablespoons dried shrimp, or 60 g (2 oz) fresh prawns (shrimp)

1 tablespoon Pepper and Coriander Paste (*page 23*)

1 teaspoon finely chopped garlic

1 tablespoon fish sauce

1 teaspoon palm sugar

125 g (4 oz) minced (ground) pork

4 banana capsicums (sweet peppers)

Pork - stuffed capsicum in egg net
(Prik Sod Sai Rum)

An appetiser on its own, or part of the range of accompaniments served with Iced Rice (*page 150*).
Makes 4

Make the egg nets first and leave them to cool. Beat the eggs, water and salt together. Puncture several fine holes in the base of a clean empty can or plastic food container. Lightly grease a heated wok or frying pan. Fill the can with the egg mixture and make a light egg net by criss-crossing the base of the pan. Use low heat because the egg net should not become brown. When set, loosen the net with a spatula or knife, then carefully lift off and lay on a plate. Repeat with the remaining mixture.

If using dried shrimp, soak in hot water for 10 minutes, then drain and chop. Pound the prawns, pepper and coriander paste, garlic, fish sauce and palm sugar, or chop in a food processor. Add to the pork mince and mix well.

Cut the stem end off each capsicum and with a pointed knife carefully remove all seeds. Pack with the pork mixture, using a small spoon. Replace the stem end and steam for 10–15 minutes. Allow to cool for a few minutes, wrap with the egg nets, and serve with chilli sauce and a cucumber salad.

1 cup (4 oz) rice flour

¼ cup (1 oz) tapioca flour

¼ teaspoon salt

2 tablespoons oil

1 cup (8 fl oz) water

crushed fried garlic (optional)

Filling:

125 g (4 oz) minced (ground) pork

250 g (8 oz) chicken fillets, minced (ground)

3 tablespoons oil

1 medium onion, finely chopped

1 tablespoon Pepper and Coriander Paste (*page 23*), or 2 teaspoons finely chopped garlic
  2 tablespoons finely chopped fresh coriander (cilantro/Chinese parsley), including roots
  ½ teaspoon black peppercorns, crushed

2 or 3 small hot chillies, finely chopped

1 tablespoon fish sauce

1 tablespoon palm sugar

3 tablespoons roasted salted peanuts, crushed

red chilli slices

Steamed dumplings with pork and chicken
(Khanom Jeeb)

These pitcher-shaped dumplings should be small enough to eat in one mouthful. Season the filling with sufficient emphasis so it is not neutralised by the blandness of the dough. A popular garnish and flavour accent is added by sprinkling the dumplings with crushed fried garlic just before serving. Serve extra garlic separately, for those who wish to indulge.
Makes about 20

Note:
Fried garlic for sprinkling is most easily made by frying some dried garlic flakes on gentle heat. Since these burn easily, lift them out on a strainer as soon as they are a pale gold colour. Drain on absorbent paper and when cool and crisp, crush lightly. Put the fried garlic in a small sauce dish and hand it around with the dumplings.

Combine the rice and tapioca flours, salt, oil and water in a saucepan and stir over moderate heat until it becomes a paste. Turn it into a bowl and when cool enough to handle, knead to a smooth paste. Divide it into 20 small balls, cover with a damp cloth and leave aside while preparing the filling.

Filling:
Combine the pork and chicken. Heat the oil and fry the onion, stirring frequently, until it softens. Add the pepper and coriander paste, or the garlic, coriander and peppercorns. Stir-fry until fragrant. Add the pork and chicken and stir to break up any lumps. Keep frying until the meats are well cooked, then add the chillies, fish sauce and palm sugar. Stir constantly until the liquid has evaporated. Turn onto a plate to cool and mix in the peanuts.

    With floured hands mould the balls of dough into small cup shapes. Place a teaspoonful of filling inside each and gather the edges together to seal. Pinch off any excess dough and flatten the top of each dumpling. Using a fine metal skewer, mark with lines all round to decorate. Place on oiled greaseproof (non-stick baking) paper and steam for 20 minutes. After 5 minutes, lift the dumplings onto the serving plate and garnish each one with a slice of red chilli.

Steamed dumplings with pork and chicken, Galloping horses.

250 g (8 oz) minced (ground) pork or pork chop
2 teaspoons finely chopped garlic
1 tablespoon chopped fresh coriander (cilantro/Chinese parsley) roots
¼ teaspoon black pepper
2 tablespoons oil
¼ cup (1 oz) dry-roasted peanuts, crushed
1–2 tablespoons fish sauce
3 tablespoons palm sugar
1 fresh red chilli, seeded and chopped
2 tablespoons chopped fresh coriander leaves and stems
approximately 24 orange or mandarin segments

Galloping horses (Fruit with savoury topping)
(Ma Ho)

It's a curious name, but so well known that if you're ordering in a Thai restaurant this is what you should ask for. Or go one better and use its Thai name – *Ma ho.*
Makes about 24

If using a pork chop, trim off the skin and bone, and chop meat very finely. Pound the garlic, coriander roots and black pepper together in a mortar and pestle or, if you have some already made up, use a tablespoon of Pepper and Coriander Paste (*page 23*) instead.

Heat the oil in a wok or frying pan and on low heat fry the mixture until it smells fragrant. Add the pork and fry until it changes colour. Add the peanuts, fish sauce, palm sugar, chilli and coriander and continue to stir-fry until the mixture is well cooked, dark brown and quite dry.

Segment the oranges or mandarins. Slit through the membrane and flesh and open the segments flat, removing any seeds. Place a spoonful of pork on each piece of fruit. Thin slices of pineapple may be used instead if convenient.

½ cup dried shrimp

1 cup soaked fine rice noodles

1 or 2 sliced chillies

2 teaspoons fish sauce

1 teaspoon lime juice or
vinegar

1 teaspoon sugar

1 tablespoon shredded dried
radish

8 rice paper sheets

16 small cooked prawns
(shrimp), shelled and
deveined

about 48 basil leaves

8 small pieces of lettuce

lettuce leaves

shredded carrot and giant
white radish

Clear sauce:

4 tablespoons sugar

½ cup (4 fl oz) cold water

2 tablespoons fish sauce

finely sliced red and green
chilli

1 tablespoon lime juice or
vinegar

Fresh spring rolls
(Poh Pia)

These are fresh spring rolls, the rice paper wrapping pliable and transparent instead of crisp-fried and golden brown – an ideal low-fat version of the popular snack.
Makes 8

Soak the dried shrimp in hot water for 10 minutes, drain and chop. Measure out the fine rice noodles after soaking them in hot water for 10 minutes. Drain them well and chop into short lengths. Mix the shrimp and noodles with the chillies, fish sauce, lime juice and sugar. Simmer the shredded radish in water for 5 minutes, drain and add to the mixture.

Dip a sheet of rice paper in warm water and lay on a flat surface. Place 2 prawns on one side of the rice paper and then a heaped tablespoon of the noodle mixture. Cover with about 6 basil leaves and a small piece of lettuce. Bring the ends of the rice paper up and roll up, enclosing the filling firmly, then arrange on lettuce leaves with the prawns showing through on top and the seam underneath.

Garnish with fine shreds of carrot and giant white radish, and serve with a clear sauce.

Stir the sugar and cold water until the sugar dissolves, then add the remaining ingredients. This method gives a very clear, glossy sauce.

 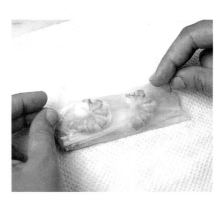

2 large sheets dried bean curd
skin

250 g (8 oz) raw prawns
(shrimp)

1 tablespoon cornflour
(cornstarch)

2 tablespoons finely diced
pork fat

½ teaspoon crushed garlic

½ teaspoon salt

½ teaspoon finely grated fresh
ginger

¼ teaspoon ground black
pepper

oil for deep-frying

Prawn rolls
(Hae Gun)

Dried bean curd skin is used to wrap these tasty rolls.
Makes about 12 slices

Soak the bean curd skin in warm water until soft, then drain. Shell and devein the prawns and chop finely. Mix the prawns, cornflour, pork fat, garlic, salt, ginger and pepper thoroughly. Divide into two equal portions and shape each into a roll. Place a roll on each sheet of bean curd skin and roll up tightly. Put into a steamer over boiling water and steam for 10 minutes. Allow to become cold, then deep-fry until brown. Cut into diagonal slices and serve with a dipping sauce.

Fresh spring rolls

300 g (10 oz) white fish fillets

2 teaspoons Red Curry Paste
(*page 20*)

1 tablespoon fish sauce

2 tablespoons cornflour
(cornstarch)

1 egg, beaten

1 teaspoon finely chopped red
chilli

2 tablespoons chopped spring
onions (scallions)

½ cup finely sliced green
beans

oil for frying

Shallow-fried fish cakes
(Tod Mun Pla)

A characteristic of these fish cakes is their bouncy texture. Use a firm white fish such as ling or cod.
Makes 6

Remove any trace of skin or bone from the fish fillets and cut into small pieces. Put into a food processor fitted with a steel blade and process until smooth. Add the red curry paste, fish sauce, cornflour and egg. Process again until well combined.

With a spatula, scrape the fish paste into a bowl and stir in the red chilli, spring onions and beans. Heat oil in a frying pan to 1 cm (½ in) deep. With oiled hands form ¼ cup portions of the mixture into flat round cakes on an oiled frying spatula. Slide the fish cakes into the hot oil, a few at a time, and fry on medium heat until deep golden brown underneath. Turn the cakes over carefully and fry until the other side is done to the same golden brown colour. Remove with a slotted spoon and drain on absorbent paper. Serve warm or cold with Chilli and Cucumber Salad (*page 39*).

Shallow-fried fish cakes,
Chilli and cucumber salad,
Water chestnut 'apples', Young corn
with prawns, and Cracker balls

20 water chestnuts

Pomelo Salad (*page 66*), or small quantity other savoury filling

chilli or murraya leaves

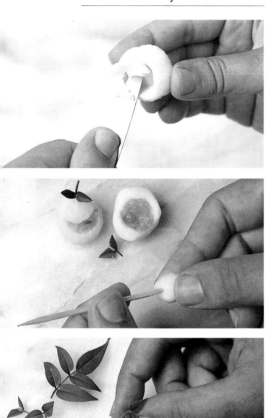

Water chestnut 'apples'
('Apple' Haeo)

Being invited to a party at Bangkok's famous Oriental Hotel is more than an extremely pleasurable experience, it is an education. Among the dainty appetisers offered to us were hollowed-out water chestnuts filled with tangy pomelo salad, the lids garnished with stem and leaves so they looked like bite-sized apples. These may be filled with other mixtures, such as the savoury pork filling in Steamed Sago Balls (*page 44*), or the chicken filling from Golden Cups (*page 45*).
Makes 20

If fresh water chestnuts are available, peel them and slice off the tops, then hollow out the centres with a small knife. Since fresh water chestnuts are not easy to come by, we used canned chestnuts, selecting the largest and best shaped. Although flattened at top and bottom, a more rounded effect is achieved if the tops are taken out in a slightly conical shape and inverted when being replaced. Hollow out the centre a little more to make room for the filling.

Fill with pomelo salad or one of the savoury mixtures mentioned above. A practical way is to save a little of the filling from any of the recipes. You will need only about a quarter of the recipe quantity as the chestnuts don't hold very much. For this reason, emphasise the flavour of the filling. If using the pomelo salad, separate the fruit segments into small pieces, taking care not to crush them, and add more salt and chilli than if serving as a salad.

With a wooden toothpick make a small hole in the conical side of the lid of each water chestnut so it is easy to insert the decorative stem and leaves. Trim some chilli leaves, murraya or other non-toxic leaves to size with scissors and push into place.

250 g (8 oz) raw prawn (shrimp) meat

1 egg white

1 tablespoon fish sauce

2 teaspoons Pepper and Coriander Paste (*page 23*)

4 tablespoons finely sliced spring onions (scallions), or chopped shallots

1–2 teaspoons finely chopped red chillies

fresh or canned young corn cobs

Young corn with prawns
(Goong Haw Hao Poad)

A variation on the recipe on page 47. If the price of prawns is soaring, use a mixture of prawns and fish.
Makes about 12

Devein the prawns and place in a blender with the egg white, fish sauce, pepper and coriander paste and half the spring onions, and reduce to a paste; or chop the prawns finely and beat with a wooden spoon until paste-like. Mix in the remaining spring onions and the chillies so the prawn paste will be prettily flecked with colour. With wet hands mould the mixture around the corn cobs as described in the recipe on page 47 and steam for 8–10 minutes, or until the prawn mixture changes colour.

250 g (8 oz) minced (ground) pork
125 g (4 oz) raw prawns (shrimp), deveined and chopped, or 125 g (4 oz) flaked crab meat
½ teaspoon black peppercorns
1 teaspoon finely chopped garlic
½ teaspoon salt
4 tablespoons finely chopped fresh coriander (cilantro/Chinese parsley), including roots
¼ teaspoon finely grated kaffir lime rind
1 tablespoon fish sauce
1 egg, beaten
1 tablespoon cornflour (cornstarch)
half a sheet bean curd skin
spring onion (scallion) tops, or garlic chives
oil for frying

Chilli sauce:

½ cup (4 fl oz) white vinegar
3 red chillies, seeded and sliced
2 teaspoons finely chopped garlic
½ cup (4 oz) sugar
½ teaspoon salt
1 tablespoon fish sauce

Cracker balls
(Pratad Lom)

The name is a direct translation from the Thai, and these are little squares of bean curd skin with a filling of savoury pork and prawn mixture, gathered up and tied, first steamed and finally deep-fried. *Makes about 16*

Put the pork and prawns or crab into a bowl. Crush the peppercorns with a mortar and pestle, add the garlic, salt, coriander and lime rind, and pound to a paste. Mix into the pork and prawns together with the fish sauce, egg and cornflour until thoroughly combined.

Soak the bean curd skin in warm water for a few minutes, drain, and cut into 10 cm (4 in) squares. Split the spring onion tops; if using chives, leave whole. Pour boiling water over them and leave for a minute until flexible. Drain on absorbent paper.

Place a tablespoon of the pork mixture in the centre of a square of bean curd skin. Gather the top and tie with an onion top. Continue until all the filling is used. Steam over fast-boiling water for 10 minutes, remove from heat and cool. The cracker balls may be prepared ahead up to this point and refrigerated.

Shortly before serving, heat the oil in a wok and deep-fry a few balls at a time until golden brown and crisp. Drain on absorbent paper and serve warm with a dipping sauce such as Chilli Sauce (*see below*).

Place the vinegar, chillies and garlic in a blender and blend at high speed, then pour into a saucepan. Add the sugar and salt and boil for 3–5 minutes. Add the fish sauce and allow to cool.

2 tablespoons sugar
2 tablespoons water
2 tablespoons fish sauce
2 tablespoons lime juice
½ cup finely sliced cucumber
2 tablespoons sliced purple shallots
1 red chilli, sliced

Chilli and cucumber salad
(Nam Jim Tang Guar)

A small relish-type salad to accompany any appetisers.

Stir the sugar with the water, fish sauce and lime juice until dissolved. Add the cucumber, shallots and chilli.

Dough:

1 cup (4 oz) gluten-free flour (wheat starch)
3 tablespoons cornflour (cornstarch)
¾ cup (6 fl oz) boiling water
1 tablespoon oil
¼ teaspoon salt

Filling:

1 tablespoon oil
1 large onion, finely chopped
2 teaspoons Pepper and Coriander Paste (*page 23*)
500 g (1 lb) minced (ground) pork
3 teaspoons palm sugar
2 tablespoons fish sauce
½ cup (2 oz) crushed roasted peanuts
crushed roasted peanuts, or crushed fried garlic flakes (*page 209*)

125 g (4 oz) minced (ground) pork
125 g (4 oz) chicken thigh fillets, skin removed
125 g (4 oz) cooked and flaked crab meat
2 tablespoons chopped fresh coriander (cilantro/Chinese parsley), including roots
¼ teaspoon ground black pepper
2 teaspoons chopped garlic
2 tablespoons finely chopped spring onions (scallions)
2 tablespoons fish sauce
2 tablespoons thick coconut milk
2 small eggs
2 red chillies, sliced
fresh coriander leaves

Steamed pork dumplings
(Khanom Jeeb Moo)

Makes about 24

Dough:

Sift the flours into a bowl. In a small saucepan bring the water to the boil. Add the oil and salt and pour onto the flour, stirring constantly with a wooden spoon. When cool enough to handle, knead lightly until smooth.

Shape the dough into a cylinder about 2.5 cm (1 in) in diameter and divide into 1 cm (½ in) slices. Wrap in plastic film to prevent the surface drying out. Take one piece at a time and roll out to a circle 8 cm (3 in) in diameter. Moisten one edge with water. Place 1 teaspoonful of pork mixture in the centre and fold over. Pinch the edges of the dough together decoratively. Place the dumplings on a lightly oiled plate and steam until transparent, about 15–20 minutes. Sprinkle with extra crushed peanuts or crushed fried garlic and serve hot with a salad.

Filling:

Heat the oil and stir-fry the onion until soft. Add the pepper and coriander paste and cook until fragrant. Add the minced pork and cook, stirring, for 10–15 minutes or until tender. Add sugar, fish sauce and peanuts and cool before filling the dumplings.

Fat horses
(Ma Uon)

I suppose these may be described as bite-sized terrines, steamed in tiny moulds. If possible, shape cups from banana leaves but, more realistically, use foil confectionery cups or the small wine cups sold in Asian supermarkets.
Makes about 16

Put the pork and diced chicken meat into a food processor. Pick over the crab meat and discard any bits of cartilage or shell. Pound the fresh coriander, pepper and garlic to a paste. Add to the meats and process until smooth. Remove to a bowl and mix in the crab meat, spring onions, fish sauce and coconut milk.

Beat one egg and the white of the second egg together and add to the mixture. Press into small cups, smoothing the tops. Stir the yolk of the second egg and brush the tops with it. Steam over boiling water for 20 minutes, cool and remove from the cups. Garnish each with a slice of chilli and a couple of coriander leaves.

Prawn-filled omelette

250 g (8 oz) prawns (shrimp), shelled and deveined

2 teaspoons Pepper and Coriander Paste (*page 23*)

2 spring onions (scallions), sliced

2 tablespoons oil

3 large eggs

2 tablespoons water

salt and white pepper

2 red chillies, shredded

sprigs of coriander (cilantro/Chinese parsley)

strips of chilli

Prawn-filled omelette
(Kai Yad Sai Goong)

Makes 10–12

Chop the prawns and mix with the pepper and coriander paste and spring onions. Heat 1 tablespoon of the oil and stir-fry the prawns for 2 or 3 minutes. Turn onto a plate and set aside.

Beat the eggs slightly with the water, and add salt and pepper to taste. Heat an omelette pan, lightly grease it with some of the remaining oil and cook batches of 2 tablespoons of egg at a time to make small omelettes. Cook over low heat and do not let them brown. Turn, cooked side down, onto a plate. Repeat until all the mixture is used.

Place a tablespoon of the prawn mixture in the centre of each omelette and top with a few shreds of chilli and a coriander leaf. Fold in the ends of the omelette and roll up to enclose the filling. Garnish with chilli strips (dipped in hot water to make them pliable) and coriander sprigs. Serve with a dipping sauce if you like.

250 g (8 oz) white fish fillets
1 tablespoon Red Curry Paste (*page 20*)
2 tablespoons finely chopped spring onions (scallions)
1 teaspoon finely chopped lime rind
½ teaspoon crushed garlic
2 teaspoons fish sauce
⅛ teaspoon ground black pepper
2 fresh red chillies, sliced
spring onion tops

Moulded fish cakes
(Look Chin Pla)

The first time I encountered these was at a small, exclusive restaurant in Bangkok where palace cuisine was served. The tiny fish seemed to swim in their sea of green lettuce. The fragrance of lime rind, the pungency of garlic, chillies and pepper ensure these are no ordinary fish cakes.
Makes 12 fish cakes

Remove any skin and bones from the fish and cut into pieces. Put through a mincer, chop very finely or grind in a food processor, adding all the other ingredients except the chillies and spring onion tops. Oil 12 small moulds and press the fish mixture into them. Place in a steamer and steam over boiling water for 10 minutes, or until firm and opaque. Allow to cool slightly before turning out. Decorate with slices of chilli and spring onion tops, and serve warm or cold.

Note:
If you haven't any fish-shaped moulds, use scallop shells which may be bought very cheaply at fish markets. The shell shapes are pretty, though not quite as cute as the little fish.

500 g (1 lb) small mussels
125 g (4 oz) pork mince (ground pork)
2 teaspoons Pepper and Coriander Paste (*page 23*), or Red Curry Paste (*page 20*)
1 tablespoon finely chopped lemon grass
½ teaspoon grated kaffir lime rind
2 tablespoons thinly sliced spring onions (scallions)
2 teaspoons cornflour (cornstarch)
2 teaspoons fish sauce
1 teaspoon palm sugar
1 egg white
fine shreds of kaffir lime leaf and red chilli

Steamed stuffed mussels
(Hoi Mangpoo Mok)

If preferred, use 125 g (4 oz) fish fillets or prawn meat instead of the pork to make the savoury topping for the mussels.
Serves 4

Scrub the mussels well with a brush under cold water. Beard the mussels by giving a sharp tug at the brown fibres protruding from the shells. The mussel shells should be tightly shut – discard any which are not. Place the mussels on a rack and steam just until the shells open, discarding any which remain closed. Remove the top shells and discard.

Combine the pork and the next 8 ingredients, mixing well. Top each mussel with a heaped teaspoon of the mixture, smoothing it over the mussel. Place fine shreds of lime leaf and chilli on each and arrange in a steamer. Steam over boiling water for 15 minutes, or until cooked and firm. Serve warm or cold.

Moulded fish cakes

1½ cups (8 oz) sago

¾ cup (6 fl oz) hot water

¼ teaspoon salt

½ cup (2 oz) tapioca flour

Filling:

2 coriander (cilantro/Chinese parsley) plants

3 large cloves garlic

½ teaspoon whole black peppercorns, or 2 teaspoons Pepper and Coriander Paste (*page 23*)

1 medium onion

2 tablespoons oil

250 g (8 oz) lean minced (ground) pork

3 teaspoons palm sugar, or brown sugar

2 tablespoons fish sauce

⅓ cup crushed roasted peanuts, or crunchy peanut butter

To serve:

2 teaspoons crushed fried garlic flakes (*page 209*), or crushed roasted peanuts

lettuce leaves

chilli flowers

Pork-filled sago balls
(Saku Sai Moo)

These glistening, translucent little mouthfuls are not only pretty to look at but wonderfully savoury to eat. Serve as an appetiser with pre-dinner drinks or put them on the table as a preliminary to the main dishes. If the recipe makes more than required, the extras may be frozen and steamed when needed.
Makes about 60 balls

Rinse the sago in a fine strainer, transfer to a bowl and gradually mix in the hot water in which the salt has been dissolved. Mix well, cover and stand for an hour.

Filling:
Roughly chop the coriander roots and stems and the garlic, pound to a paste in a mortar and pestle, then remove to a plate. Pound the black peppercorns until coarsely crushed. Finely chop the onion.

Heat the oil in a wok or frying pan and cook the coriander-garlic paste and the onion over low heat until soft. Add the peppercorns or pepper and coriander paste, and cook until the mixture starts to brown.

Add the pork, increase heat and fry, pressing the meat with the back of the spoon to prevent lumping. Cook until browned. Reduce heat to medium, add the palm sugar and fish sauce and stir well. Cover and cook on low heat until the pork is tender and liquid all absorbed. Stir frequently to ensure the mixture doesn't stick and burn. Remove from heat, stir in the peanuts or peanut butter, and allow to cool slightly.

To cook the balls:
With a wet spoon take equal amounts of sago and roll into balls with damp hands. Cover with a damp cloth. Wash and dry your hands and dust with tapioca flour. Hollow out each ball into a cup shape, put in small teaspoonfuls of pork mixture and seal the sago over the filling. Mould into balls again and set aside, covered.

Place the balls on oiled paper strips in a steamer, leaving some space between as they increase slightly in size. Steam over fast-boiling water for 15–20 minutes or until the sago is quite clear. Remove the steamer from the heat and allow to stand for about 5 minutes for the balls to dry slightly before transferring to the serving dish. Sprinkle with crushed fried garlic or roasted peanuts, and garnish with chilli flowers. Serve hot.

Batter:

¼ cup (1 oz) rice flour
¼ cup (1 oz) wheat flour
¼ cup (2 fl oz) canned coconut milk
¼ cup (2 fl oz) water
1 teaspoon sugar
oil for deep-frying

Filling:

1 clove garlic
2 coriander (cilantro/Chinese parsley) roots
1 small onion
1 tablespoon oil
125 g (4 oz) minced (ground) pork or chicken
1 red chilli, sliced
2 spring onions (scallions), finely chopped
1 tablespoon chopped pickled garlic
2 teaspoons fish sauce
1 teaspoon palm sugar
1 tablespoon lime juice
1 tablespoon crushed roasted peanuts
fresh coriander leaves
2 tablespoons corn kernels

Golden cups
(Krathong Tong)

Crisp, light batter in a flower shape holds a savoury mixture and is named for the lotus-shaped floats which are so much a part of the *Loy Krathong* Festival, the biggest celebration of the year in Thailand. *Makes about 30*

Batter:
Combine both kinds of flour with the coconut milk and water, stirring to a thick, smooth batter. If necessary add an extra tablespoon of water to give a batter which will coat the mould. Stir in the sugar.

Heat oil for deep-frying in a small pan. Prepare a special *krathong* mould, or improvise one. The mould is a fluted metal shape attached to a wooden handle (*see page 24*). I find a fluted tartlet tin grasped firmly with metal tongs works very well as an alternative.

Heat the mould in the oil, then lift it out and let the oil drain for a second or two. Dip it into the batter, being careful not to immerse the top of the mould or the batter will not detach from it. Return it to the oil and hold it until the cup fries and floats free. Lift from the oil onto absorbent paper when golden. (The cups may be made ahead and stored in an airtight container when completely cold.) Make the filling and cool to room temperature. Fill the cups just before serving for maximum crispness.

Filling:
Pound the garlic, coriander roots and onion together. Heat the oil and on gentle heat fry the mixture until fragrant and starting to turn golden. Add the meat and fry, stirring, until it changes colour. Add the remaining filling ingredients, except for the coriander leaves and corn kernels, and continue to cook, stirring frequently, for 10 minutes. Cool. Fill the cups and garnish with coriander leaves and corn kernels.

Pork-filled sago balls (before and after steaming)

Leaf lilies
(Miang Cha Plu)

1 bunch *cha plu* leaves, or
  1 butter lettuce

2 teaspoons Red Curry Paste
  (*page 20*)

2 tablespoons coconut milk

2 tablespoons chopped spring
  onions (scallions)

90 g (3 oz) minced (ground)
  pork

60 g (2 oz) flaked cooked
  crab meat

1 tablespoon finely chopped
  coriander (cilantro/Chinese
  parsley) leaves

1 tablespoon crushed roasted
  peanuts

1 teaspoon palm sugar

1 teaspoon chopped red chilli

½ cup cold cooked rice

1 teaspoon finely chopped
  kaffir lime leaves

a few fine strips of red
  chillies

The leaf known as *Cha plu* (*Piper sarmentosum*) is an attractive, glossy leaf with a tangy flavour. It is filled with tasty mixtures and sold as a snack. If the leaves are soaked in water with a little sugar added to keep them in good condition, I have discovered that not only do they stay fresh, they also take on a slightly sweet and most pleasant flavour. You can substitute butter lettuce or any other pliable leaf that can be eaten without cooking.
Makes about 30

Wash the *cha plu* leaves and soak for at least 2 hours in cold water with a couple of spoonfuls of sugar dissolved in it. The leaves may be soaked overnight.

Heat together the red curry paste and coconut milk, stirring. Add the spring onions and pork, and stir-fry until the pork is cooked. Remove from heat and mix in the crab meat, coriander leaves, crushed peanuts, palm sugar, chopped chilli and rice.

Drain the *cha plu* leaves, blot dry on a clean tea towel and place a spoonful of the mixture near the stem. Roll each into a lily shape and fasten with a toothpick. Garnish with lime leaves and chilli strips. Serve with a dipping sauce. Remove the toothpick, fold the lily into a little parcel, dip and eat.

Note:
If preferred, fill the leaves with a mixture of toasted coconut and dried shrimp pounded together and moistened with lime juice, crushed roasted peanuts, finely chopped fresh ginger and small shallots, a little sugar and some sliced fresh, hot chilli.

Young corn cobs with steamed fish
(Pla Haw Kao Poad)

1 x 455 g (14½ oz) can young
  corn cobs, or 1 dozen fresh
  mini cobs

250 g (8 oz) white fish fillets

¼ teaspoon white pepper

2 teaspoons chopped garlic

1 tablespoon chopped
  coriander (cilantro/Chinese
  parsley) roots

1 teaspoon chopped galangal,
  or ½ teaspoon ground

2 tablespoons finely sliced
  lemon grass, or 1 strip
  lemon rind, chopped

1 tablespoon fish sauce

2 tablespoons finely chopped
  spring onions (scallions)

2 teaspoons finely chopped
  red chillies

If fresh corn is available it needs no pre-cooking; the steaming will be sufficient. If using canned corn, drain the cobs well and pat dry on kitchen paper towels.
Serves 6

Drain the canned corn and blot dry on paper towels; remove the husks and corn silk from fresh cobs.

Remove any skin and bones from the fish and chop very finely, or put into a food processor with the pepper. Pound the garlic, coriander roots, galangal and lemon grass or rind to a paste, or reduce to a paste in a blender, adding the fish sauce to facilitate blending. Add to the fish with the spring onions and chillies and mix well.

Divide evenly into 12 portions and mould around the centre of each corn cob, firming on carefully and leaving both ends uncovered. Place in an oiled steamer and steam over boiling water for 8–10 minutes. Serve with a dipping sauce or salad.

Leaf lilies

Pumpkin and coconut soup

Soups

In a Thai meal soups are not served as a first course, as in Western meals. Instead, the bowl of soup comes together with other dishes, to be sipped throughout the meal or spooned over rice to moisten it. These are generally light, clear soups.

On the other hand, there are soups which *are* the meal. Bowls laden with noodles of various kinds, and just a few slices of meat or some prawns.

There are soups which are gently seasoned and others which will awaken your tastebuds with a jolt. A quantity of chilli, which blends and merges with other spices in a curry eaten with rice, can catch you by the throat when swallowed by the spoonful, so be wary. At the same time, don't allow yourself to be scared away from the tingling, refreshing flavours of such national favourites as Hot and Sour Prawn Soup, the famous *Tom Yum Goong*. There is also the mild and equally delicious Chicken with Galangal, a creamy coconut milk soup with the fragrance of fresh herbs.

1.5 litres (6 cups) water
1 large onion
1 large carrot
5 thin slices fresh ginger
5 coriander (cilantro/Chinese parsley) roots and attached stems
a few celery leaves (optional)
500 g (1 lb) chicken necks and backs, or beef or pork bones
1 teaspoon salt
½ teaspoon whole black peppercorns

Soup stock

Bring the water to the boil while preparing the other ingredients. Peel and quarter the onion and scrape the carrot. Put into the boiling water together with all the other ingredients. Return to the boil, then lower heat, cover and simmer for 45 minutes to 1 hour. Strain and use right away, or cool and chill, then remove any fat from the surface and freeze for future use.

500 g (1 lb) ripe pumpkin, peeled and cubed
1 tablespoon lime or lemon juice
2 teaspoons dried tamarind pulp
½ cup (4 fl oz) hot water
½ cup dried shrimp
½ cup chopped onions or shallots
3 or 4 red chillies, chopped
1 stalk lemon grass, finely chopped
1 teaspoon dried shrimp paste
2 cups (16 fl oz) thin coconut milk
1 cup (8 fl oz) thick coconut milk
½ cup basil leaves
1 tablespoon fish sauce
1 cup (8 fl oz) chicken stock or water

Pumpkin and coconut soup
(Gaeng Liang Fak Thong)

A rich, delightfully flavoured soup. If 'pumpkin soup' conjures up a taste-memory of Western-style pumpkin soup, you are in for a surprise!
Serves 6

Place the pumpkin in a bowl and sprinkle with the lime juice. Soak the dried tamarind in the hot water for 10 minutes, squeeze to dissolve the pulp and strain through a nylon sieve. Set aside for later.

Soak the dried shrimp in some hot water for 10 minutes, then drain. Pound together with the onions, chillies, lemon grass and shrimp paste; or place these ingredients in a food processor or blender and reduce to a paste.

Put the paste into a saucepan with the thin coconut milk and stir until boiling. Simmer 5 minutes. Stir in the tamarind liquid and pumpkin, stir again and simmer 10 minutes, or until pumpkin is tender. Stir in the thick coconut milk and basil leaves and bring back to the boil, adding fish sauce to taste. If necessary thin the soup a little with chicken stock or water.

Note:
Ripe pumpkin is brightly coloured, firm textured and sweet in flavour. An unripe pumpkin has none of these desirable characteristics. It is better to buy it in the piece so you can judge the colour — even experts can't tell how ripe it is until it is cut.

Prawn soup with mushrooms

60 g (2 oz) bean starch noodles

24 dried lily buds

6 dried *shiitake* mushrooms

2 teaspoons finely chopped garlic

½ cup chopped fresh coriander (cilantro/Chinese parsley), including roots

375 g (12 oz) raw prawns (shrimp)

3 tablespoons peanut oil

1.5 litres (6 cups) water

1 medium onion, finely sliced

4 spring onions (scallions), sliced finely

2 tablespoons fish sauce

1 teaspoon sugar

fresh coriander leaves

Prawn soup with mushrooms
(Kaeng Chud Goong Hed)

A mild soup in which the flavours are those of prawns, dried *shiitake* mushrooms and garlic.
Serves 6

Put the noodles in a bowl and pour boiling water over them to cover. Leave to soak. In another bowl soak the lily buds and the dried mushrooms in hot water for 30 minutes. Pinch off the hard ends of the lily buds and tie a knot in each one. Cut off the tough stems of the mushrooms and slice the caps thinly. Cut the noodles into short lengths.

Pound the garlic and coriander together, or put into an electric blender with a little water and purée.

Shell and devein the prawns and use the heads and shells to make a stock. To do this, first fry them in a tablespoon of the oil in a large saucepan, then add the 1.5 litres water and simmer for 20 minutes. Strain the stock.

Heat the remaining oil and fry the onion until soft and translucent, stirring now and then. Add the garlic and coriander purée and fry, stirring constantly, over medium heat until it is fragrant. Add the prawns and fry until they change colour, then pour in the hot stock, lily buds, mushroom slices and noodles. Bring the soup to the boil, simmer gently for 5 minutes, then stir in the spring onions, fish sauce and sugar. Taste and adjust the seasoning. Serve garnished with fresh coriander leaves.

1.25 litres (5 cups) Soup Stock
(*page 50*)

1 tablespoon oil

2 teaspoons Pepper and
Coriander Paste (*page 23*)

1 teaspoon chopped garlic
crushed with 2 teaspoons
sugar

250 g (8 oz) Meatballs
(*page 136*)

2 dried kaffir lime leaves

½ cup spring onions
(scallions), cut into short
lengths

2 tablespoons fish sauce

90 g (3 oz) canned young
corn cobs, drained

125 g (4 oz) rice noodles,
soaked in hot water for
10 minutes

1 chilli, finely sliced

1–2 tablespoons lime or
lemon juice

Soup:

1.5 litres (6 cups) chicken or
pork Soup Stock (*page 50*)

2 kaffir lime leaves

1 tablespoon sugar

1 clove garlic, crushed

1 tablespoon fish sauce

2 tablespoons lime juice

1 teaspoon Tom Yum Paste
(*page 22*)

Cucumber flowers:

2 small green cucumbers

125 g (4 oz) finely minced
(ground) pork

2 teaspoons fish sauce

1 small clove garlic, crushed

⅛ teaspoon ground black
pepper

1 strip kaffir lime rind, finely
chopped

Sour soup with meatballs
(Tom Yum Look Chin)

Refreshingly piquant but not too hot, this soup may be served on its
own as a first course if you wish.
Serves 4

Make and strain the stock. Heat the oil and fry the pepper and
coriander paste until fragrant. Add the crushed garlic and sugar and
stir in the stock. Bring to the boil, then drop in the meatballs
(prepare as in recipe on *page 136*, but do not fry). Add the lime leaves
and simmer for 10 minutes.

Add all remaining ingredients except the lime juice and simmer
5 minutes longer. Add enough lime juice to give a slightly sour
taste.

Soup with cucumber flowers
(Tom Yum Tang Yud Sai)

Thai food has a delicate and beautiful look, even something as
commonplace as a bowl of soup — take this one for example. And
cucumber flowers are not difficult to make.
Serves 6

Put all the ingredients for the soup into a stainless steel or enamel
pan and simmer, covered, while preparing the cucumber flowers.
Carefully place the flowers in the liquid, base downwards, and
simmer gently for 8–10 minutes, just until the pork balls are cooked.

Cucumber flowers:
Cut the cucumbers crosswise into short lengths and with a sharp
knife shape one end like the petals of a flower. Scoop out some of
the seeds with a small spoon, but leave enough to form the base of
the cup. Combine the rest of the ingredients and mix well. Form
into small balls and place one in each cucumber section.

*Sour soup with meatballs and soup
with cucumber 'flowers'*

6 slices fresh, frozen or dried galangal
1 small roasting chicken
3 cups (24 fl oz) thin coconut milk
¼ teaspoon black pepper
3 fresh coriander (cilantro,/ Chinese parsley) roots, crushed
2 stems lemon grass, thinly sliced
3 fresh green chillies
1½ teaspoons salt
3 or 4 fresh or frozen kaffir lime leaves
1 cup (8 fl oz) thick coconut milk
1 tablespoon fish sauce
lime juice to taste
3 tablespoons chopped fresh coriander leaves

Chicken and galangal in coconut milk
(Tom Kha Gai)

A distinctive soup which is probably one of the two most popular in Thai cuisine. The other is *Tom Yum Goong*, Hot Prawn Soup. This, by contrast, is creamy rich with coconut milk, and the predominant flavour is that of the aromatic rhizome, galangal.
Serves 6

If using dried galangal, soak it in hot water to cover for 30 minutes. Cut the chicken into serving pieces and put into a saucepan with the thin coconut milk, galangal, pepper, coriander roots, lemon grass, whole chillies, salt and lime leaves.

Bring to the boil over low heat. Simmer, uncovered, until the chicken is tender, stirring occasionally. Add the thick coconut milk and stir constantly until it returns to the boil. Remove from heat and stir in the fish sauce and lime juice.

Serve sprinkled with chopped coriander leaves and accompanied with steamed rice.

⅓ cup dried shrimp
5 coriander (cilantro/Chinese parsley) roots
2 teaspoons chopped garlic
1 teaspoon dried shrimp paste
¾ cup chopped onions
1.25 litres (5 cups) Soup Stock (*page 50*)
4 cups prepared vegetables such as bamboo shoot, beans, straw mushrooms, young corn cobs, zucchini (courgettes)
2 tablespoons fish sauce
1 teaspoon palm sugar
½ cup sweet basil or coriander leaves

Mixed vegetable soup
(Kaeng Liang Pak)

A mild, clear vegetable soup flavoured with shrimp.
Serves 6

Soak the dried shrimp in hot water for 10 minutes. Put into a blender or food processor with the coriander roots, garlic, shrimp paste and onions. Add a little water if necessary and blend to a purée.

Add the paste to the stock and bring to the boil. Add the vegetables to the stock, putting in those which require longer cooking first and the quick-cooking ones last. Stir in the fish sauce and palm sugar, and throw in the basil or coriander leaves at the last minute. Serve hot.

Note:
If Pepper and Coriander Paste (*page 23*) is already made and in the refrigerator, 2 teaspoons may be substituted for the coriander roots and garlic, but the soup will be a darker colour.

Chicken and galangal in coconut milk and mixed vegetable soup

Hot sour prawn soup

(Tom Yum Goong)

500 g (1 lb) medium-sized raw prawns (shrimp)

1 tablespoon oil

2 litres (8 cups) water

1 teaspoon salt

2 stems fresh lemon grass, thinly sliced, or 4 strips thinly peeled lemon rind

4 fresh, frozen or dried kaffir lime leaves

4 slices galangal, fresh or frozen

2 or 3 fresh chillies

2 teaspoons chopped garlic

1–2 tablespoons fish sauce

3 tablespoons lime juice

1 fresh red chilli, seeded and sliced

2 tablespoons chopped coriander (cilantro/Chinese parsley) leaves

4 spring onions (scallions) with green tops, chopped

This is the best known Thai soup, and one which really wakes up the tastebuds . . . lots of lime juice and chillies are essential, as are other fresh herbs such as lemon grass and lime leaves.
Serves 6

Shell and devein the prawns, save the heads and shells and dry them on kitchen paper. Heat the oil in a saucepan and fry the heads and shells until they turn red. Add the water, salt, lemon grass, lime leaves, galangal, chillies and garlic. Bring to the boil, cover and simmer for 20 minutes. Strain the stock.

Return to the saucepan and add the prawns, then simmer for 3–4 minutes or until the prawns are cooked. Add the fish sauce and lime juice to taste, and remove from the heat at once. Serve in a tureen or in soup plates, sprinkled with the sliced chilli, and the chopped coriander leaves and spring onions.

Note:
Instead of having to scramble around for the ingredients each time you make this, whenever you have them all make a batch of *Tom Yum Paste* (*page 22*), which lasts for weeks in the refrigerator. Then a bowl of this tangy soup will take only as long as boiling the water! Just stir 3 tablespoons *tom yum paste* into 1.25–1.5 litres (5–6 cups) boiling stock or water, drop in the prawns and simmer only until they turn pink. Garnish and serve.

Hot sour seafood soup

(Tom Yum Ta-Leh)

125 g (4 oz) fresh raw prawns (shrimp)

1 tablespoon oil

1 teaspoon dried shrimp paste

1 tablespoon Pepper and Coriander Paste (*page 23*)

4 dried or frozen kaffir lime leaves

1 red chilli, split and seeded

2 stalks lemon grass, very thinly sliced diagonally

1.5 litres (6 cups) fish or prawn stock

1 cup shredded cabbage, or sliced beans

125 g (4 oz) fish fillets

2 spring onions (scallions)

1 tablespoon lime or lemon juice

1 tablespoon fish sauce

2 teaspoons palm sugar

sliced red chilli

More than slightly pungent, depending on the strength of the chilli used in the soup. Some are hotter than others, and as a general rule the smaller the chilli, the hotter it is. Serve this with plain white rice.
Serves 4

Shell the prawns, reserving the heads and shells. Devein the prawns, rinse quickly and dry on kitchen paper.

Heat the oil and fry the prawn heads and shells until pink. Add the shrimp paste and pepper and coriander paste, and stir-fry for 1 minute. Add the kaffir lime leaves, chilli, lemon grass and stock and simmer for 15 minutes. Strain and return the liquid to the saucepan with the shredded cabbage or sliced beans. Simmer 10 minutes longer.

Add the fish and prawns and simmer a further 4 or 5 minutes, just until the fish turns white and opaque, and the prawns pink. Stir in the spring onions, lime juice, fish sauce and palm sugar. Serve in bowls, garnished with slices of red chilli.

Hot sour seafood soup and hot sour prawn soup

375 g (12 oz) lean rump or round steak

2 teaspoons Pepper and Coriander Paste (*page 23*)

½ teaspoon grated kaffir lime rind

1 litre (4 cups) thin coconut milk

2 stems lemon grass, very thinly sliced

5 slices fresh or frozen galangal, thinly sliced

3 frozen or dried kaffir lime leaves

1 cup (8 fl oz) thick coconut milk

½ cup spring onions (scallions), sliced

2 or 3 sliced chillies

2 teaspoons palm sugar

1–2 tablespoons fish sauce

4 tablespoons chopped fresh coriander (cilantro/Chinese parsley)

Beef soup with coconut milk
(Tom Kha Nuer)

This soup remains spicy enough to spoon over rice, even though its 'bite' is tempered by coconut milk and palm sugar.
Serves 6

Trim any fat or sinews from the beef and cut into very thin strips. Combine the pepper and coriander paste, lime rind and beef strips, mix well and leave to marinate for 10–15 minutes.

Bring the thin coconut milk to the boil, stirring constantly. Add the beef, lemon grass, galangal and lime leaves and stir until it returns to the boil. Reduce heat and simmer, uncovered, 30 minutes or until the meat is tender. Mix in the thick coconut milk, spring onions, chillies, palm sugar and fish sauce. Top with fresh coriander.

Note:
For a lighter soup, part of the coconut milk may be replaced by water or a light stock. If fresh lime leaves are available, remove the central leaf ribs and shred the leaves very finely. Dried leaves are used whole.

Beef soup with coconut milk

12 medium-sized dried *shiitake* mushrooms

125 g (4 oz) minced (ground) pork, or chopped raw prawns (shrimp)

1 teaspoon finely chopped garlic

3 spring onions (scallions), finely chopped

1 tablespoon finely chopped coriander (cilantro/Chinese parsley)

1 tablespoon Golden Mountain Sauce (*see Glossary, page 202*)

¼ teaspoon ground black pepper

1 tablespoon finely chopped water chestnuts

1.5 litres (6 cups) chicken Soup Stock (*page 50*), defatted

half a green cucumber

1 tablespoon fish sauce, or to taste

chilli slices (optional)

Mild soup with stuffed mushrooms
(Kaeng Chud Hed Yud Sai)

Timid about hot flavours? Then this is a good dish to try.
Serves 6

Pour very hot water onto the mushrooms in a bowl and leave to soak for 30 minutes. Squeeze out excess water and cut off the stems — these may be simmered in the stock for extra flavour but should be removed before serving the soup.

Combine the pork or prawns (or a mixture of both) with the garlic, 2 tablespoons of the chopped spring onions, the coriander, Golden Mountain sauce, pepper and water chestnuts. Mix well.

Pack the mixture into the drained mushroom caps and cook for 15−20 minutes in 3 cups (24 fl oz) of the chicken stock. (If dropped into deep stock the mushrooms tumble over and the filling falls out, but this won't happen once the filling is cooked.) Peel the cucumber and cut in halves lengthwise, remove the seeds and slice crosswise.

Just before serving, place 2 mushrooms in each soup plate. Add the remaining stock, the cucumbers and the fish sauce to the pan and simmer for 3 or 4 minutes. Ladle over the mushrooms and garnish with the remaining spring onions and some chilli slices if you like.

Mild soup with stuffed mushrooms

250 g (8 oz) fresh straw or button mushrooms

1.5 litres (6 cups) water

1 teaspoon salt

2 stems fresh lemon grass, thinly sliced, or 4 strips thinly peeled lemon rind

4 fresh, frozen or dried kaffir lime leaves

4 slices galangal, fresh or frozen

2 or 3 fresh chillies

2 teaspoons chopped garlic

1 cup (8 fl oz) thick coconut milk

1–2 tablespoons fish sauce

3 tablespoons lime juice

1 fresh red chilli, seeded and sliced

2 tablespoons chopped coriander (cilantro/Chinese parsley)

4 spring onions (scallions) with green tops, chopped

---

6 chicken drumsticks, skin removed

1 teaspoon chopped garlic

3 or 4 red chillies, seeded and sliced

1 tablespoon Pepper and Coriander Paste (*page 23*)

1.5 litres (6 cups) chicken Soup Stock (*page 50*)

2 fresh, frozen or dried kaffir lime leaves

¾ cup chopped onions or shallots

3 slices fresh or frozen galangal

2 stems lemon grass, finely sliced

2 teaspoons sugar

2 tablespoons fish sauce

2 tablespoons lime juice, strained

chopped fresh coriander (cilantro/Chinese parsley)

sliced chillies (optional)

Mushroom *tom yum*
(Tom Yum Hed)

Mushrooms are very much part of the Thai diet, and straw mushrooms, in particular, are plentiful in Thailand. Those used in our photograph were given to me by Dr Yip Cho, of Sydney University, who is pioneering mushroom research in Australia. By the time this book is on sale, it's very likely that fresh straw mushrooms should be available here, too. The mushrooms on the plate alongside the bowl of soup include golden mushrooms, also the subject of research, and oyster mushrooms, a variety which is now grown commercially in Australia.
Serves 6

Wipe the mushrooms and if using straw mushrooms, bring them to the boil in a pan of lightly salted water and simmer for 3 minutes, then drain. Straw mushrooms should always be blanched like this, and may then be stored in the refrigerator for up to a week.

Put the water, salt, lemon grass, lime leaves, galangal, chillies and garlic into a saucepan. Bring to the boil, cover and simmer for 20 minutes. Add the mushrooms and simmer for a further 5 minutes.

Stir in the coconut milk. Add the fish sauce and the lime juice to taste, then remove from the heat at once. Serve in a tureen or in soup plates, sprinkled with the sliced red chilli, the coriander leaves and spring onions.

Sour and spicy chicken soup
(Tom Yum Gai)

The name says it all — so temper the spiciness with steamed rice.
Serves 6

Chop each drumstick in two. Pound the garlic, chillies and pepper and coriander paste together, and mix with the chicken pieces. Allow to marinate for 15 minutes.

Place the stock, lime leaves, onions, galangal, lemon grass and sugar in a large saucepan, add the chicken and simmer for 30 minutes, or until the chicken is very tender. Add the fish sauce and lime juice. Check the flavour, which should be spicy and sour. Serve with coriander leaves sprinkled over, and extra sliced chillies if you like it really hot.

Note:
If you have some *Tom Yum* Paste (*page 22*) in the refrigerator or freezer, a quick way to make this soup is to use a tablespoon of paste to marinate the chicken.

Mushroom tom yum

1.5 litres (6 cups) chicken Soup Stock (*page 50*)
1 whole chicken breast
2 teaspoons Pepper and Coriander Paste (*page 23*)
2 teaspoons fish sauce
1 cup fresh bean sprouts, trimmed
½ cup sliced spring onions (scallions)
125 g (4 oz) rice vermicelli, soaked for 10 minutes in hot water
1 or 2 sliced red or green chillies
coriander cilantro/Chinese parsley) leaves to garnish

Chicken and noodle soup
(Sen Mee Gai)

Nothing like its namesake which comes out of a packet, this one has real slices of chicken and the tang of fresh herbs.
Serves 6

Make the stock, and when it is almost ready slide the chicken breast into the pan and simmer very gently for 6–8 minutes. Turn off the heat and let the chicken remain in the liquid until quite cool, then remove any skin and bones and with a sharp knife cut the meat into neat slices.

Reheat the stock and stir in the pepper and coriander paste, fish sauce, bean sprouts and the spring onions. Add the drained rice vermicelli and heat through, stir in the chicken slices and serve garnished with chilli slices and coriander leaves.

Chicken and noodle soup

3 dried *shiitake* mushrooms

90 g (3 oz) pork

90 g (3 oz) chicken breast fillet

90 g (3 oz) raw prawns (shrimp)

60 g (2 oz) bean starch noodles

1 tablespoon chopped fresh coriander (cilantro/Chinese parsley)

½ teaspoon black peppercorns

1 teaspoon finely chopped garlic

1 tablespoon oil

1.5 litres (6 cups) pork or chicken Soup Stock (*page 50*), or prawn stock

1 tablespoon Golden Mountain Sauce (*see* Glossary, *page 202*)

1 tablespoon fish sauce

6 spring onions (scallions), sliced

1 small green cucumber, peeled, seeded and sliced

1 egg, very lightly beaten

Garnish:

sliced chilli, chopped fresh coriander, or spring onion tops

Combination soup
(Kaeng Chud Ruam Mit)

The differing tastes of pork, chicken, prawns and vegetables give this soup a variety of textures and flavours. If you prefer it mild, omit the sliced chilli.
Serves 4–6

Soak the dried mushrooms in hot water for 30 minutes. Squeeze out excess moisture, discard the stems and slice the caps.

Slice the pork into thin strips. Cut the chicken into slices. Devein the prawns and cut in halves if large. Soak the bean starch noodles in hot water for 10–15 minutes, drain and cut into short lengths.

Pound the coriander, peppercorns and garlic together, or use 2 teaspoons Pepper and Coriander Paste (*page 23*). Heat the oil and fry the pounded mixture, stirring, until fragrant. Add the pork and chicken and stir-fry until the colour changes. Add the stock, Golden Mountain sauce, fish sauce, mushrooms and noodles, and simmer for 15 minutes.

Stir in the spring onions, cucumber and prawns, and cook for 3 or 4 minutes. Slowly dribble in the egg, stirring lightly as it sets. Sprinkle with sliced chilli, chopped coriander or spring onion tops.

---

125 g (4 oz) lean pork

6 dried *shiitake* mushrooms

125 g (4 oz) raw prawns (shrimp)

2 chillies (optional)

1 tablespoon oil

1 tablespoon Pepper and Coriander Paste (*page 23*)

1.25 litres (5 cups) chicken or pork Soup Stock (*page 50*)

2 kaffir lime leaves

1–2 tablespoons fish sauce

1 teaspoon palm sugar

coriander (cilantro/Chinese parsley) leaves

Pork and mushroom soup
(Kaeng Chud Moo Hed)

Not too hot, and for an even milder flavour, skip the chillies.
Serves 6

Dice the pork and set aside. Soak the mushrooms in hot water for 30 minutes to soften. Remove the stems and discard. Slice the mushroom caps. Shell and devein the prawns, seed and slice the chillies.

Heat the oil and fry the pepper and coriander paste, add the diced pork and stir-fry until the colour changes. Add the stock and lime leaves and simmer for 25 minutes, until the pork is tender.

Add the mushrooms and chillies and cook for 10 minutes, then add the prawns and cook for 3 minutes more. Flavour with the fish sauce and palm sugar, and garnish with coriander leaves before serving.

Salads, Sauces and Dips

A Thai salad can be cool, refreshing and pungent, all at once.

On my trips to Thailand I've been fascinated by the numerous leaves, roots and shoots that are eaten raw, dipped in one or other of the hot sauces. Thais are very keen on raw vegetables and include them in the daily diet both for their food value and taste.

Alongside the vegetables will be the essential Thai dipping sauce, *Nam Prik*. There is not just one, but many variations of this. The word '*nam*' means water, and '*prik*' means chilli, so it doesn't take much imagination to know it will be rather hot. In most mixtures, however, there is enough palm sugar to take the edge off the pungent chilli and make the sauce a pleasantly stimulating experience.

Bean starch noodle salad with water chestnuts

50 g (1½ oz) bean starch noodles
8–10 dried chillies
⅓ cup dried shrimp
1 stem lemon grass
½ teaspoon chopped garlic
½ teaspoon sugar
1 tablespoon fish sauce
2 tablespoons lime juice
2 teaspoons palm sugar
¾ cup sliced water chestnuts
½ cup sliced spring onions (scallions)
a sprig of basil
a sprig of coriander (cilantro/Chinese parsley)

Bean starch noodle salad with water chestnuts
(Yum Woon Sen Gub Haeo Chin)

Because the fine, transparent noodles made of mung bean starch are so difficult to cut when they are dry, I suggest you buy them in 50 g (1½ oz) skeins, usually six to a large pack. It is easy then to use just one small bundle instead of having to cut off a small amount from a large skein.
Serves 4–6

Soak the bean starch noodles in hot water for 10 minutes to soften. Break off the tops of the chillies and shake out the seeds. With scissors, snip the chillies into large pieces, then soak with the dried shrimp in warm water for 10 minutes to soften. Slice the lemon grass very finely, using only the tender portion. Crush the garlic with the sugar.

Put the chillies, shrimp, garlic and lemon grass in a blender with a little of the chilli-prawn soaking water and blend until smooth. Mix in the fish sauce, lime juice and palm sugar and set aside.

Test the noodles for tenderness and if they are still somewhat chewy, boil them for a few minutes until quite transparent and tender. Drain and cut into short lengths. Combine with the water chestnuts, spring onions and lemon grass. Add the blended shrimp mixture and toss to mix thoroughly. Serve garnished with basil and coriander leaves.

1 pomelo, or 2 grapefruit
1 small clove garlic
1 red chilli, seeded and sliced
1 tablespoon palm sugar
1 tablespoon fish sauce
2 tablespoons lime juice
¼ cup dried shrimp, reduced to a floss in an electric blender
2 tablespoons pea-sized eggplants (aubergines) (optional)
1 stem lemon grass, sliced very finely

Pomelo salad

(Yum Som-O)

Pomelo may be an unfamiliar fruit in Western countries at present but that looks set to change. It resembles a giant grapefruit and, like grapefruit, there are pink and white varieties. It is now being imported into Australia, and has probably been available in Europe for quite some time — I have seen exotic fruits of many varieties for sale in England, Switzerland and Holland. But don't fret if it has not reached your local market yet, as grapefruit may be substituted.
Serves 4

With a sharp knife peel the fruit, taking off all the thick skin and laying bare the flesh. Divide into segments by cutting between the membranes. Remove any seeds and put the segments in a bowl.

Crush the garlic or pound in a mortar with half the sliced chilli, the palm sugar, fish sauce and lime juice. Mix in the shrimp floss, eggplants if used, and the lemon grass and pour over the pomelo or grapefruit segments in the bowl. Add the remaining chilli slices. Toss gently, then transfer to a serving plate.

Green pawpaw salad,
Pomelo salad

2 cups finely shredded green pawpaw (papaya)
½ cup tender green beans, sliced (use snake beans if available)
2 tablespoons dried shrimp
2 tablespoons crushed roasted peanuts

Dressing:

1 small clove garlic
2 purple shallots, or 1 small brown onion
2 fresh chillies
2 teaspoons fish sauce
1 tablespoon raw sugar, or palm sugar
2 tablespoons lime juice, or to taste

Green pawpaw salad

(Som Tam)

Now readily available where fresh Asian ingredients are sold, the green pawpaw or papaya used in this salad is not merely slightly under-ripe, it is very green indeed, and the flesh is quite white (*see* photograph, *page 67*). Very popular in Thailand, some stalls are devoted solely to this salad. Each order is freshly made, the ingredients being combined and lightly pounded in a mortar and pestle.
Serves 4

Peel the pawpaw and shred the flesh very finely — the grating attachment on a food processor will make short work of the job; otherwise use a grater, making the strands as long as possible. String the beans and cut them into bite-sized pieces. Put the dried shrimp in a food processor or blender and grind finely, then combine with the roasted peanuts.

In a mortar and pestle pound the garlic, shallots, chillies, fish sauce and sugar. Add the beans and pound gently so they don't lose their shape, then the pawpaw shreds and pound lightly. Add the lime juice and toss together. Pile onto a plate and sprinkle the dried shrimp and the peanuts over.

a few lettuce leaves
1 mango
1 orange
half a ruby grapefruit
half a white grapefruit
half a ripe pineapple
½ cup water chestnuts
a few miniature tomatoes
a few seedless grapes
1 cup cooked, sliced chicken
1 cup cooked, shelled prawns

Dressing:

4 tablespoons sugar
½ cup (4 fl oz) cold water
2 tablespoons fish sauce
1 tablespoon lime juice
1 red chilli, seeded and sliced
1 small clove garlic, crushed

Garnish:

¼ cup crisp-fried shallots
1 teaspoon crisp-fried garlic flakes, crushed (*page 209*)
¼ cup roasted salted peanuts, crushed

Mixed fruit salad with chicken and prawns

(Yum Polamai)

A salty, sour, slightly hot dressing brings out flavours in familiar fruit that you never dreamed were there! I have used a selection of fruit in season — substitute whichever varieties are available.
Serves 6

Wash and dry the lettuce leaves. Peel and slice the mango. Peel and segment the orange and lay the segments carefully on a plate lined with lettuce leaves. Do the same with the grapefruit.

Use a sharp, stainless steel knife to peel the pineapple. Quarter lengthwise and trim off the tough core, then cut across into thin slices. If the water chestnuts are whole, slice them into rounds. Wash and chill the tomatoes. Wash the grapes and halve them if they are large. Combine the chicken and prawns in a small bowl. Mix the dressing ingredients together and sprinkle a tablespoonful over the chicken and prawns, tossing to distribute the flavours. Put the rest of the dressing in the bowl in which it will be served, and place on the platter with the fruit so that each person may spoon some over their portion.

Sprinkle the crisply fried shallots, garlic and roasted peanuts over the salad just before serving.

Dressing:
Dissolve the sugar in the cold water, then add the remaining ingredients.

Red cabbage salad, Mixed fruit salad with chicken and prawns

1 cup finely sliced onion
1 tablespoon salt
¼ cup dried shrimp
2 cups finely shredded red cabbage
2 cups finely shredded green or white cabbage
2 teaspoons palm sugar
2–3 tablespoons lime juice
1 teaspoon Pepper and Coriander Paste (*page 23*)
2 teaspoons fish sauce, or to taste
lettuce leaves
small whole chillies

Red cabbage salad
(Yum Kalum Plee)

Serves 4–6

Put the sliced onion in a bowl, rub the salt into the onions and leave for 20 minutes. Soak the dried shrimp in hot water for 10 minutes and remove any sandy streaks.

Lightly pound the drained, soaked shrimp and add 1 cup each of the red and green cabbage. Rinse the salted onions in cold water, drain well, and rub or mix in the sugar, lime juice, pepper and coriander paste and fish sauce. Combine all the ingredients and mix well. Serve on lettuce leaves, garnished with chillies.

12 large raw prawns (jumbo shrimp)
salt
4 tablespoons (3 fl oz) lime juice
1 small red onion, finely sliced
2 red chillies, seeded and sliced
1 cup (8 fl oz) thick coconut milk
1 teaspoon rice flour
1 red chilli
2 or 3 fresh kaffir lime leaves

Prawn salad in coconut milk
(Yum Goong Kati)

A refreshing cold dish to serve either as a first course or along with the rice and other main dishes.
Serves 4–6

Shell the prawns, removing all but the last segment of shell and the tail. With a sharp knife slit each along the curve of the back and remove the vein. Rinse the prawns and rub well with salt. Bring a small pan of water to the boil, drop the prawns in and cook for less than 1 minute, or just until they turn opaque and curl. Remove from the heat at once, lift out with a slotted spoon and place in a bowl with the lime juice and a few slices of the onion and chillies. Mix well and set aside until cold.

Heat the coconut milk in a small saucepan. Stir in the rice flour mixed with a tablespoon of the coconut milk and cook until it thickens slightly. Pour into a bowl and cool. Drain the liquid from the prawns and stir it into the coconut milk. There should be enough lime juice and salt to season the milk, but if necessary add a pinch of salt and a squeeze of lime juice.

Arrange the prawns on a serving plate and pour the coconut milk dressing over and around them. Pile the rest of the onion and chillies in the centre and garnish with fine strips of red chilli and kaffir lime leaves.

Mango salad

2 firm mangoes, or green apples
½ teaspoon salt
1 tablespoon peanut oil
2 teaspoons dried garlic flakes
4 spring onions (scallions), thinly sliced
125 g (4 oz) pork fillet (tenderloin), finely chopped
1 tablespoon dried shrimp, reduced to a floss in an electric blender
1 tablespoon fish sauce
1 tablespoon lime juice
1 teaspoon palm sugar
2 tablespoons crushed roasted peanuts
1 or 2 red chillies, finely sliced

Mango salad

(Yum Ma Muang)

If you have access to unripe or half-ripe mangoes, this is a seasonal treat. You can, however, enjoy this refreshing salad all year round by substituting tart cooking apples.
Serves 4

Peel the fruit and slice thinly, then cut the slices into julienne strips and put into a large bowl. If using apples, add the lime juice now to prevent discolouring. Sprinkle with salt and toss gently.

Heat the oil and fry the garlic until pale golden, lift out and drain. In the same oil fry the spring onions and set aside. Quickly fry the pork until cooked and brown, add the shrimp floss, fish sauce, lime juice (if using mangoes), and palm sugar. Just before serving put everything together in the bowl, toss lightly and garnish with the peanuts and chillies.

Chicken and cucumber salad
(Yum Gai Taeng Gwa)

A light and refreshing salad, ideal for dieters.
Serves 4

250 g (8 oz) chicken breast

1 large or 2 small green cucumbers

2 red chillies

1 tablespoon dried shrimp

2 tablespoons fish sauce

2 tablespoons lime juice

1–2 teaspoons sugar

lettuce leaves

fresh mint leaves (optional)

Steam the chicken breast and when cool remove the skin and slice the meat. Peel the cucumbers, or leave the skin on if tender. Slice thinly. Remove the seeds from the chillies, then slice finely. In a blender reduce the dried shrimp to a floss.

In a small bowl combine the fish sauce, lime juice and sugar, and toss gently with the chicken, cucumbers and chillies. Serve on lettuce leaves and sprinkle the shrimp floss over. A few tender young mint leaves may be added if you like.

Seafood salad
(Yum Ta-Leh)

The secret to tender seafood is short cooking. Even half a minute too long can be critical, so watch carefully and act quickly!
Serves 4

250 g (8 oz) raw prawns (shrimp)

250 g (8 oz) cleaned squid

2 kaffir lime leaves

2 sprigs coriander (cilantro/ Chinese parsley)

1 stem lemon grass, finely sliced

1 tablespoon fish sauce

2 tablespoons lime juice

2 teaspoons palm sugar

1 teaspoon crushed garlic

1 teaspoon finely chopped fresh ginger

½ teaspoon black pepper

½ cup finely sliced spring onions (scallions), including some green tops

¼ cup lightly packed mint leaves

2 or 3 fresh red chillies, finely sliced

Shell and devein the prawns. Leave the tails on for colour if liked. Slit the squid tubes and rinse. Rub clean with kitchen paper and use a sharp knife to score the inside surface diagonally in parallel lines. Hold the knife at an angle of 45 degrees to achieve deep cuts. Cut the squid into 4 cm (1½ in) strips and then into 5 cm (2 in) pieces.

In a small saucepan boil 2 or 3 cups (16–24 fl oz) water with the lime leaves, coriander and lemon grass for 5 minutes. Drop in the squid and as soon as the pieces curl and turn opaque and white, lift them out on a slotted spoon. It should take less than a minute. Drop in the prawns too, only until they turn pink, then lift out immediately.

Stir together the fish sauce, lime juice, palm sugar, garlic, ginger and pepper. Toss the seafood in the dressing, then add the fresh herbs and chillies and mix lightly.

Note:
If the squid you buy is very large and might be tough, tenderise it by marinating for some hours in half a teaspoon of bicarbonate of soda (baking soda) dissolved in 3 tablespoons of hot water.

500 g (1 lb) fish fillets
2 onions
3 red tomatoes
2 tablespoons vinegar
2 tablespoons fish sauce
2 tablespoons hot chilli sauce
1 tablespoon palm sugar
3 tablespoons oil
roughly chopped fresh coriander (cilantro/Chinese parsley)
finely sliced red chillies

Fish in chilli-tomato sauce
(Pla Saus Makua Tet)

Serves 4

Rinse and dry the fish. Chop the onions finely. Peel, seed and chop the tomatoes. In a small bowl mix together the vinegar, fish sauce, chilli sauce and palm sugar, stirring to dissolve the sugar.

Heat the oil and fry the onions over moderate heat, stirring frequently, until soft and starting to turn golden. Add the tomatoes and the vinegar mixture, cover and simmer for 15–20 minutes, until the sauce is thick. Add the fish fillets, spooning the sauce over them. Cover and cook gently until the fish is done. Garnish with chopped coriander and sliced red chillies. Serve with rice.

2 fillets or cutlets of your choice of fish
½ cup (4 fl oz) coconut milk
2 teaspoons rice flour
¼ teaspoon salt
1 tablespoon lime or lemon juice
2 teaspoons fish sauce
a few slices red chilli, seeds removed
finely sliced spring onion (scallion)
chopped coriander (cilantro/ Chinese parsley)

Fish with coconut cream sauce
(Pla Ob Kati)

Serves 2

The fish may be steamed, grilled (broiled), microwaved or fried, whichever method is most convenient. Cook it until just done, don't overcook.

In a small pan stir over low heat the coconut milk, rice flour and salt until thickened. Sprinkle the fish with the lime juice and fish sauce and spoon over the coconut milk mixture, then garnish with the chilli and spring onion slices and the chopped coriander leaves.

Lobster and mandarin salad
(Yum Goong Gub Som)

1 small cooked lobster

50 g (1½ oz) bean starch noodles

2 large pieces dried wood fungus

2 large mandarins or oranges

3 tablespoons fish sauce

2 tablespoons sugar

2 tablespoons lime juice

1 teaspoon chopped red chilli

¼ cup roasted, crushed peanuts

2 tablespoons crisp fried shallots

2 teaspoons fried garlic (optional)

small bunch watercress

few sprigs of fresh coriander (cilantro, Chinese parsley)

chilli flower

If lobster is a bit rich for the budget, substitute prawns, seafood flakes or any other delicate seafood in season.
Serves 4–6

With a sharp knife cut into the lobster from underneath, remove the meat and cut 6 thin slices for garnish. Shred the rest of the lobster meat. Boil the bean starch noodles in lightly salted water for about 10 minutes, until soft and transparent. Drain and cut into short lengths. Soak the wood fungus for 10 minutes in hot water, then cut into fine strips. Peel the mandarins or oranges, divide into segments and remove all the membranes.

Combine the fish sauce, sugar, lime juice and chopped chilli, stirring to dissolve the sugar. Pour the mixture over the lobster, noodles and wood fungus, add the crushed peanuts and fried shallots and toss to distribute flavours. Taste and add more fish sauce or lime juice if desired. Chill until required.

To serve the salad, pile on a platter lined with washed and dried watercress or lettuce. If the lobster is a particularly handsome specimen use the empty shell as a focal point and place the salad alongside. Arrange the reserved lobster slices and mandarin segments on top and garnish with coriander sprigs and a chilli flower.

Rose petal salad

(Yum Dok Gulab)

4 or 5 roses

1 steamed chicken breast

1 cup small cooked prawns

1 cup slivers of cooked pork

2 tablespoons very fine shreds of pork skin from Sweet Pork (*page 126*)

6 segments of pomelo or pink grapefruit

¼ cup crushed roasted peanuts

2 teaspoons crisply fried garlic

1 tablespoon crisply fried shallots

a few leaves of frilly lettuce

slices of cucumber

2 tablespoons fish sauce

3 teaspoons sugar

1 tablespoon lime juice

1 fresh red chilli, sliced

Use fragrant old-fashioned roses, ideally from your own garden. If you get them from anywhere else, be sure the roses have not been sprayed with pesticides. Combine seafood and meats as available, but the main flavours are those of crushed, roasted peanuts, fried garlic and the crisp-fried shallots or sliced onions readily available in Asian stores.
Serves 4–6

Wash the roses under a gentle spray of cold water, shake the water from them and place the blossoms, petals downwards, to drain on kitchen paper towels.

With a sharp knife cut the chicken breast meat into thin strips. Shell and devein the prawns and, if not very small, cut them into pieces. Combine the chicken and prawns in a bowl with the pork, pork skin, grapefruit segments, half the crushed peanuts, fried garlic and shallots. Arrange on a plate lined with lettuce and garnish with cucumber.

In a small bowl stir together the fish sauce, sugar, lime juice and chilli until the sugar dissolves. Spoon the mixture over the combined ingredients and scatter the rose petals over the top. (See the photograph on the back cover for a different way to arrange this salad: with various components in separate piles, petals placed to resemble a rose, and cucumber cut to look like leaves.) Serve the rest of the peanuts, garlic and fried shallots in a small bowl for sprinkling on top.

2 mud crabs, or 3 blue swimmers
3 red chillies
2 stems lemon grass
2 small shallots
2 tablespoons lime juice
2 teaspoons fish sauce
1 small clove garlic
1 teaspoon sugar
½ cup fresh mint sprigs
½ cup fresh coriander (cilantro/Chinese parsley)
lettuce leaves, washed and dried
lime slices and red chilli

Crab salad
(Pla-Poo)

There is no quick and easy way to make a superb crab salad. Sure, you can use frozen or canned crab but it will not look like the photograph nor will it taste anything like freshly cooked crab.

If the crabs are already cooked, remove the meat from the shells in pieces as large as possible, picking out any bits of shell and cartilage and discarding the feathery grey tissue underneath the hard top shell or carapace.

To cook live crabs, either drop them into boiling water or put them in the freezer for an hour or two and when they have lost consciousness, boil in lightly salted water for 10–15 minutes. Lift out of the water and leave to cool before attempting to crack the claws and pick the meat from the shell.

With a sharp knife cut off the stem ends of the chillies and remove the seeds, then cut in thin slices. Use only the pale, tender portion of lemon grass just above the root and slice very thinly. Cut the shallots in thin slices.

Combine the lime juice and fish sauce. Crush the garlic with the sugar to a smooth paste and stir into the lime juice mixture. If you like, a little of the chilli can be crushed or finely chopped and added to the dressing. Mix well and combine with the crab meat. Add the chillies, lemon grass and shallots, and toss very gently. Add half the mint and coriander.

Line a serving plate with lettuce leaves and place the crab meat on top. Garnish with the rest of the mint and coriander, lime slices and chilli.

1 cooked crab
1 x 185 g (6 oz) can water chestnuts
1 small onion, finely chopped
2 teaspoons chopped garlic
1 tablespoon oil
2 tablespoons fish sauce
2 tablespoons lime juice
2 teaspoons palm sugar
½ teaspoon finely grated kaffir lime rind
1 small hot chilli, finely chopped
250 g (8 oz) cooked prawns (shrimp)
250 g (8 oz) finely sliced cooked pork
¼ cup roughly chopped fresh coriander (cilantro/Chinese parsley)
3 very tender kaffir lime or citrus leaves, cut into fine threads

Crab and water chestnut salad
(Yum Poo Gub Haeo-Chin)

Serves 6–8

Pick the meat from the crab and put into a bowl. Buy sliced water chestnuts if possible, otherwise cut them in slices and then into strips.

Fry the onion and 1 teaspoon garlic in the oil on medium heat, stirring so they do not burn. When golden put them into a small bowl and add the fish sauce, lime juice, palm sugar, lime rind and chilli. Crush the remaining teaspoon of garlic and stir in.

Shell and devein the prawns and, if large, cut into small pieces. Cut the pork into strips. Combine with the crab meat, drizzle the dressing over and toss lightly. Serve sprinkled with the fresh coriander and threads of lime leaf.

500 g (1 lb) rump, fillet or sirloin steak
1 teaspoon chopped garlic
1 tablespoon chopped coriander (cilantro/Chinese parsley) roots and stalks
¼ teaspoon freshly ground black pepper, or 1 teaspoon green peppercorns
1 tablespoon palm sugar
2 teaspoons Golden Mountain Sauce (*see* Glossary, *page 202*)
1 tablespoon lime juice
2 teaspoons fish sauce
8 small purple shallots
3 or 4 red chillies
1 stem lemon grass
1 tender cucumber
¼ cup fresh mint sprigs

Beef salad

(Yum Nuer)

Probably the most popular salad on Thai restaurant menus.
Serves 6

The best flavour comes from barbecuing the steak over coals, but if this is not possible grill (broil) under a preheated griller (broiler) or roast to medium-rare. Allow to cool completely and cut in thin slices.

Pound or crush the garlic with the coriander roots and stalks, pepper and palm sugar. Stir in the Golden Mountain sauce, lime juice and fish sauce until smooth. Peel the shallots and slice very thinly. Seed and slice the chillies. Use only the tender white portion of the lemon grass and slice very thinly. Peel the cucumber, score with a fork and slice thinly. Cut in half if the slices are large.

Combine all the ingredients and toss lightly. If preferred, arrange on a platter, garnish with mint and serve the dressing separately, as I have done in the photograph, using a hollowed out section of cucumber carved like a cactus flower (*see* step-by-step photographs, *page 79*).

Beef salad

Cucumber cactus flower

A small, sharp knife with a good point, and a small melon baller or macedoine cutter are the only tools you need for this clever bit of carving.

Cut off a section of cucumber and slice off the tapered end so it will sit flat on the plate. On the larger cut surface divide the circle into five equal sections, which will be five 'petals'. Cut each one so there is a tall point flanked by two short ones. If preferred, round off the petals instead of pointing them. Just under each high petal carve a small petal. Carefully detach this bit of skin from the flesh. Or you can leave this attached and detach the surrounding skin from the cucumber. It is possible to achieve different effects.

Scoop out the seeds and soft flesh from the centre, leaving a cup which will hold the dressing. Drop the cucumber into iced water and in a short while the 'petals' will curve outwards prettily.

4 tablespoons dried shrimp
1 stem lemon grass
2 shallots, or 1 small purple onion
3 fresh red chillies
1 tablespoon sugar
4 tablespoons lime juice
1 tablespoon fish sauce

Dried shrimp salad with lemon grass
(Yum Goong Haeng)

A salty, sour, sweet, intriguing combination which goes well with rice and curry as an accompaniment. The best dried shrimp is bright salmon pink in colour.
Serves 4

Put the dried shrimp in a bowl and pour over enough hot water to cover. Leave to soak until the shrimp are softened, about 10 minutes, then pour off the water. If any have dark veins, remove them.

Use only the tender white and pale green portions of the lemon grass, and slice very finely with a sharp knife. Peel and slice the shallots or onion very finely. Split the chillies and remove the seeds with the point of a knife, being careful not to handle the cut edges. (Plastic gloves are a wise precaution when working with chillies.) Cut the chillies into slices.

Mix the sugar, lime juice and fish sauce together. Combine all the ingredients in a bowl and toss to mix. Serve garnished with a cucumber fan.

3 tablespoons small dried
shrimp

1 clove garlic

2 shallots, or small red onions

2 fresh red chillies

2 tablespoons lime juice

2 teaspoons palm sugar

2 tablespoons fish sauce

2 tablespoons water

Vegetables:

1 bunch tender green
asparagus

a handful of tender stringless
beans

2 medium-sized carrots

4 white cabbage leaves

2 or 3 spring onions
(scallions)

a few round red radishes

2 green cucumbers

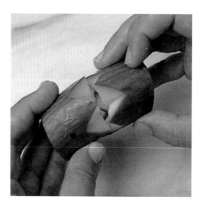

Fresh salad with *nam prik*
(Pak Nam Prik)

Nam prik is the term applied to various dipping sauces based on fish
sauce and chilli. Other ingredients may vary, but these two are
always present. The mixture may be cooked or simply mixed
together. The most useful implement in making a *nam prik* is a
primitive mortar and pestle. While electric blenders will combine a
nam prik and the flavour may be correct, the consistency is altered
and is usually too liquid. It should be thick enough to coat the raw
or lightly blanched vegetable dipped into it.
Serves 4

Look for dried shrimp which are a bright salmon pink colour and
fairly soft when pressed through the packet. This indicates they are
fresh. Those which are very hard and are a dull colour have been
around for much longer and, while they may be used, are not as
desirable.

Wash the dried shrimp and put in a shallow dish. Leave them to
soak, in just enough hot water to cover, for about 10 minutes. This
softens the shrimp sufficiently to allow any sandy veins to be
removed. Put the drained shrimp into a mortar with the garlic,
shallots and chillies, all cut into pieces. Pound steadily for a few
minutes until mashed to a paste. Gradually stir in the lime juice,
palm sugar, fish sauce and water. Serve in a small bowl with a
selection of vegetables in season to be dipped in the *nam prik* and
eaten as an appetiser.

Vegetables:
Wash the asparagus thoroughly, snap off any tough ends, and peel
the bottom half of each spear to ensure it will be tender and edible
from tip to base. Blanch in a pan of boiling water for 3 or 4 minutes
only – they should be tender but still have some snap to them. Lift
from the boiling water and plunge into a bowl of iced water to set
the colour and stop the cooking. When cold, drain. Cook the beans
in the same way and refresh in cold water.

Peel the carrots and with a sharp knife make small V-shaped
cuts at regular intervals down the length of each carrot, then cut
into round slices which will have the appearance of flowers. Cut the
cabbage into small round shapes.

Cut the spring onions into short lengths and slit the ends with a
strong pin. Drop into iced water for a few minutes and the ends will
curl. Use a thin-bladed knife to make cuts at regular intervals
around the radishes. Drop them into iced water and the 'petals' will
open.

Cut the ends off the cucumbers, then cut into tulip shapes
with a sharp, pointed knife. Make leaves from the rest of the
cucumbers, some with the skin on and others peeled. Cut oblong
slices, avoiding the seeds in the centre. Shape with a sharp knife and
use the point of the knife for leaf markings. (*See* step-by-step
photographs) Arrange all vegetables on a plate, cover with plastic
film and refrigerate until serving time.

Salad with nam prik,
Pork-filled sago balls

4 slender eggplants (aubergines)
1 teaspoon finely chopped garlic
2 teaspoons sugar
½ teaspoon salt
1–2 tablespoons lime juice
1 tablespoon fish sauce
¼ cup dried shrimp
1 red chilli, finely chopped fresh coriander (cilantro/Chinese parsley)

Grilled eggplant and dried shrimp salad
(Yum Makua Pao)

The smoky flavour eggplant acquires when grilled is the distinctive feature of this combination.
Serves 4–6

Wash and dry the eggplants. Prick them well and remove the calyxes. Spear the eggplants on a long fork and hold above a gas flame until charred all over, or cut in halves lengthways and char under the griller (broiler). Set aside until cool enough to handle, then carefully remove all skin and lay the halves on a dish, flat side down.

Crush the garlic to a paste with the sugar and salt. Add the lime juice and fish sauce and stir to dissolve the sugar. Taste the dressing – it should be sweet, sour and salty. Sprinkle the eggplants with dressing, gently lifting the edge of each eggplant half so that the dressing can flow underneath.

Pick over the dried shrimp, removing any dark spots. In an electric blender or food processor, reduce the shrimp to a floss. Sprinkle over the eggplants, leaving the rounded ends showing. Scatter chopped chilli over and garnish with sprigs of coriander. Serve warm or at room temperature.

2 large cloves garlic
3 purple shallots, or 1 small brown onion
5 fresh hot chillies
½ cup dried shrimp
2 teaspoons shrimp paste
1 tablespoon sugar
1 tablespoon palm sugar
2 tablespoons lime juice
1 tablespoon fish sauce

Nam Prik Phuket

In a small coffee shop in Phuket I had some peasant-style food, robustly flavoured and satisfying. The lady who owned and ran the shop was pleased by my interest and demonstrated this particularly delicious dipping sauce.
Serves 4

Peel the garlic and shallots, roughly chop the onion, and remove the stalks from the chillies. Soak the dried shrimp in warm water for 10 minutes and drain well. Put it all into a mortar and pound to a paste with the pestle. Wrap the shrimp paste in foil, making a flat parcel, and place under a preheated griller for 5 minutes on each side.

Add the grilled shrimp paste to the mortar and pound again, then add the sugar, palm sugar, lime juice and fish sauce. Add a little water to make a thick pouring consistency.

Grilled eggplant and dried shrimp salad, Prawn salad in coconut milk

10 medium-sized dried chillies, seeded and soaked
1 cup dried shrimp
1 cup chopped onion (2 medium onions)
1–2 tablespoons chopped garlic
½ cup (4 fl oz) peanut oil
½ cup palm sugar
1–2 teaspoons tamarind pulp concentrate (*see* Glossary, *page 202*)
¼ cup (4 fl oz) water
2 tablespoons fish sauce
2 teaspoons lime juice

Shrimp dip with tamarind
(Nam Prik Pao)

Serve as a dip with Deep-Fried Rice Crackers (*page 154*), raw or lightly cooked vegetables, or as an accompaniment with rice and curries. Keeps for weeks in a glass jar in the refrigerator.
Makes about 2 cups (16 fl oz)

Break the chillies and shake out and discard the seeds. Pour boiling water over the chillies and leave to soak for 10–15 minutes.

Put the dried shrimp in an electric blender and blend on high speed, until reduced to a floss. Empty into a bowl and without washing the blender put in the drained chillies, chopped onion and garlic, and the peanut oil, and blend on high speed until puréed. Pour into a shallow pan and fry on medium heat, stirring constantly, until the oil comes to the surface.

Add the palm sugar, tamarind, water and shrimp floss and simmer a further 5 minutes, or until a thick dipping consistency. Add the fish sauce and simmer for 2–3 minutes. Remove from heat and when cool stir in the lime juice.

¾ cup (6 fl oz) coconut milk
1 teaspoon Pepper and Coriander Paste (*page 23*)
125 g (4 oz) minced (ground) pork
2 tablespoons peanut butter
2 spring onions (scallions), finely sliced
2 tablespoons fish sauce
1 teaspoon palm sugar
1 red chilli, finely sliced

Pork and peanut dip
(Moo Lon)

This dip is primarily for Deep-Fried Rice Crackers (*page 154*) but is also nice with crisp vegetables, raw or lightly cooked.
Makes about 1½ cups (12 fl oz)

Heat the coconut milk until bubbling and cook the pepper and coriander paste until fragrant. Add the minced pork and fry, stirring constantly, until it changes colour. Stir in the peanut butter, spring onions, fish sauce, palm sugar and chilli. Turn heat down and simmer for 10 minutes or until the pork is tender. If necessary, add a little water to the sauce to produce a dipping consistency.

125 g (4 oz) fresh red chillies
125 g (4 oz) sultanas (golden raisins)
4 cloves garlic, peeled
2 teaspoons chopped fresh ginger
¾ cup (6 fl oz) white vinegar
¾ cup (6 fl oz) water
1½ (12 oz) cups white sugar
2 teaspoons salt

Sweet chilli sauce
(Saus Prik Wan)

While this sauce is sweet, it is also hot. Much depends on the variety of chillies used – small chillies are very much hotter than the larger kind.
Makes about 2 cups (16 fl oz)

Wash the chillies and snip off the stalks. If you don't wish to include the seeds with their extra heat, slit and seed the chillies and put them into an electric blender or food processor with the sultanas, garlic, ginger and enough vinegar to purée the mixture.

Pour into an enamel or stainless steel saucepan and add the rest of the ingredients. Bring to the boil and simmer, stirring occasionally, until the sauce has slightly thickened. Cool, then pour into sterilised bottles and seal.

4 tablespoons sugar
½ cup (4 fl oz) cold water
2 tablespoons fish sauce
finely sliced red and green chilli
1 tablespoon lime juice or vinegar

Sweet dipping sauce

(Saus Wan)

Makes about ¾ cup (6 fl oz)

Stir the sugar with the cold water until the sugar dissolves, then add the remaining ingredients. This method gives a very clear, glossy sauce.

1 medium-sized eggplant (aubergine), about 300 g (10 oz)
1 lime
2 small purple shallots, sliced, or 2 tablespoons chopped spring onions (scallions)
¼ teaspoon crushed garlic
½ teaspoon salt, or to taste
1 teaspoon palm sugar
1 or 2 fresh red chillies, seeded and sliced

Eggplant dipping sauce

(Nam Prik Makua)

For vegetarians, this is an ideal dipping sauce to serve with the platter of raw or lightly cooked vegetables which is part of every Thai meal.
Serves 6

Have ready a stainless steel saucepan with lightly salted boiling water. With a stainless steel knife cut the eggplant in half, peel and dice it. Drop the dice into the boiling water, cover and cook for about 8 minutes or until tender. Drain.

Meanwhile, finely grate the lime rind and squeeze the juice. Put the eggplant into the container of an electric blender with the lime rind and juice, peeled shallots, garlic, salt, sugar and chillies. Blend at high speed to combine all the ingredients. Taste, and add salt or lime juice if necessary. Serve in a small bowl, surrounded by vegetables for dipping.

6–8 large dried chillies
½ cup (4 oz) sugar
½ cup (4 fl oz) white vinegar
½ teaspoon salt
3 fresh red chillies, seeded and sliced
2 teaspoons finely chopped garlic
1 tablespoon fish sauce

Chilli sauce

(Saus Prik)

Remove the stems and seeds from the dried chillies, break the chillies in pieces and soak in hot water for 10 minutes. Drain.

Place the vinegar, both the dried and fresh chillies, and the garlic in a blender and blend at high speed, then pour into a saucepan. Add the sugar and salt and boil for 10 minutes, then add the fish sauce and allow to cool.

Fish and Other Seafood

Next to rice, fish is the most important item in the Thai diet because of the bountiful harvest of the sea, rivers, flooded paddy fields and canals which are so much a part of Thailand.

Live prawns (shrimp), crabs and crayfish, squid, mussels and dozens of different kinds of fish are plentiful in Thai markets.

Salted dried seafood is sold in another section of the markets, and this is also important in the diet – not so much as a main ingredient, but as a flavouring. If garlic, coriander (cilantro/Chinese parsley), pepper and chillies are important flavours in Thai cooking, so are flavourings derived from fish and other seafood. There is fish sauce, the ubiquitous *nam pla*, found in most recipes and placed on the table as a condiment. Almost equally prominent is dried shrimp paste, or *kapi*, which is used to spark up the flavour of most dishes, including those featuring meat. Small dried shrimp are also indispensable.

Combining prawns or crab with meat is a feature of Thai cooking.

Don't let the unfamiliarity of the combination stop you trying the recipes – the flavours blend wonderfully.

Giant stuffed prawns

4 dried *shiitake* mushrooms

¼ cup (2 fl oz) vinegar

2 tablespoons sugar

⅓ cup (2½ fl oz) water

1 tablespoon light soy sauce

2 tablespoons finely sliced spring onions (scallions)

2 teaspoons cornflour (cornstarch)

1 tablespoon cold water

2 tablespoons sweet red ginger, cut into shreds

1 whole fish, about 750 g (1½ lb)

salt

plain (all-purpose) flour

peanut oil for frying

Whole fried fish with mushroom and ginger sauce
(Platod Lard Khing Hedhom)

The sauce may be prepared beforehand and reheated just before serving, while the fish is being cooked. A delicate white fish such as flounder, pomfret or snapper is best.
Serves 4

Pour boiling water over the mushrooms, cover and leave to soak and soften for 30 minutes. Discard the stems and slice the caps finely. In a stainless steel saucepan combine the sliced mushrooms, vinegar, sugar, water and soy sauce and simmer for 5 minutes. Add the spring onions, then stir in the cornflour mixed smoothly with the cold water. Keep stirring over medium heat until the sauce boils and thickens. If preparing ahead, do not add the ginger until ready to serve or it will lose some of its pretty colour. Stir in only just before spooning it over the fish.

Wash the fish thoroughly and scrub the cavity with damp kitchen paper dipped in salt. If the fish has thick flesh, score it halfway to the bone to allow heat to penetrate. Dip the fish in flour and dust off the excess. Heat oil in a wok or frying pan until smoking hot and gently slide in the fish. Fry, ladling oil over the top of the fish, for about 5 minutes. Carefully turn the fish over and fry on the other side too. Drain on absorbent paper for a few seconds, then slide the fish onto a serving dish. Spoon some of the sauce over and serve the rest in a bowl. Serve immediately.

5 large prawns (jumbo shrimp)

1 tablespoon finely chopped spring onions (scallions)

½ teaspoon Pepper and Coriander Paste (*page 23*)

⅛ teaspoon salt

2 or 3 kaffir lime leaves, finely shredded

1 red chilli, finely shredded

Sauce:

3 dried chillies

¼ cup dried shrimp

1 teaspoon chopped garlic

½ cup (4 fl oz) thick coconut milk

2 teaspoons palm sugar

1 tablespoon fish sauce

1 tablespoon lime juice

1 teaspoon tamarind pulp concentrate

Giant stuffed prawns
(Goong Sod Sai)

Sometimes it is possible to buy the giant prawns which are so popular in Thailand, and we have used these in our photograph. But the recipe adapts just as well to local king prawns.
Serves 4

Wash the prawns and split the shells down the back. Remove the vein from each prawn and with a sharp knife slit four of the prawns halfway through. Remove the fifth prawn from its shell and chop finely. Mix the prawn meat with the spring onions, pepper and coriander paste, and salt. Divide into four equal portions and stuff into the split in each prawn.

Place the prawns in a steamer and steam over boiling water for 15–20 minutes, or until the shells turn red. The legs take longer to change colour and in this time the prawns could be over-cooked. Since the legs are too fine to yield meat, remove the steamer from the heat when the prawns are cooked. Arrange on a plate and spoon the sauce over. Garnish with shreds of lime leaf and chilli, and serve with rice.

Sauce:
Discard the stalks and seeds and break the dried chillies into pieces. Soak in a little boiling water for 10 minutes until softened. Soak the dried shrimp too, in just enough hot water to cover, for 10 minutes.
Put the drained chillies, shrimp and garlic in an electric blender

and grind everything finely, adding a little coconut milk if necessary to facilitate blending; or pound in a mortar and pestle.

Heat the thick coconut milk until oily and add the blended mixture. Cook for a few minutes, stirring well. Stir in the palm sugar, fish sauce, lime juice and tamarind liquid. Gradually stir in the thin coconut milk and simmer to reduce and thicken the sauce.

Green curry of prawns
(Kaeng Khiew Wan Goong)

Serves 4

2 cups (16 fl oz) thick coconut milk

2 tablespoons Green Curry Paste (*page 21*)

375 g (12 oz) king prawns (jumbo shrimp), shelled and deveined

2 tablespoons fish sauce

2 teaspoons sugar

½ teaspoon grated kaffir lime rind, or 3 kaffir lime leaves

In a wok bring 1 cup (8 fl oz) coconut milk to the boil, heat and stir until oily. Add the green curry paste and stir until cooked and fragrant. Stir in the prawns and remaining coconut milk and simmer 5 minutes longer. Add the fish sauce, sugar and lime rind, and taste for seasoning. Serve with rice.

Whole fried fish with mushrooms and ginger sauce, Pomfret with coconut

4 blue swimmer crabs, cooked

½ cup soaked bean starch vermicelli

250 g (8 oz) raw prawns (shrimp)

250 g (8 oz) minced (ground) pork

2 tablespoons finely chopped spring onions (scallions)

1 clove garlic

½ teaspoon salt

1 egg

1 tablespoon cornflour (cornstarch)

¼ teaspoon ground black pepper

2 tablespoons chopped fresh coriander (cilantro/Chinese parsley)

½ teaspoon finely chopped red chilli

3 cups (24 fl oz) peanut oil for frying

Stuffed fried crab
(Poo Cha)

Serves 4

Carefully remove the top shell or carapace from the crabs and discard the feathery grey tissue underneath. Wash and dry the top shells. Break open the bodies and claws and remove the crab meat.

Cut the bean starch vermicelli into 2.5 cm (1 in) lengths. Shell and devein the prawns and chop finely. Put into a bowl with the pork, spring onions and crab meat.

Crush the garlic with the salt. Beat the egg and mix in the cornflour, crushed garlic, pepper, coriander and chilli. Add to the ingredients in the bowl and mix thoroughly. Fill the crab shells with the seasoned mixture.

Heat at least 3 cups of oil in a wok or frying pan and fry the crabs, ladling oil over the top. Fry on medium heat for 7 or 8 minutes, so the filling cooks through by the time it is golden brown on the surface. Drain on absorbent paper, arrange on a serving plate and garnish with chilli flowers and sprigs of fresh coriander.

500 g (1 lb) fish fillets

250 g (8 oz) green beans, or zucchini (courgettes)

1½ teaspoons cornflour (cornstarch)

1 teaspoon Pepper and Coriander Paste (*page 23*)

1½ cups (12 fl oz) coconut milk

2 tablespoons Red Curry Paste (*page 20*)

¼ cup chopped spring onions

½ cup (4 fl oz) thick coconut milk

1–2 teaspoons palm sugar

1 tablespoon lime juice

sliced chilli

fresh coriander (cilantro/ Chinese parsley)

Fish ball curry with vegetables
(Kaeng Phed Look Chin Pla, Pak)

Serves 4

Remove all skin and any bones remaining in the fish fillets. Top and tail the beans, string them and cut into thin slices. If using zucchini, cut into julienne strips.

Chop the fish finely or blend to a paste in a food processor, adding the cornflour and pepper and coriander paste. Shape teaspoonfuls of the fish mixture into balls. Place on a plate lined with non-stick paper.

Heat ¾ cup (6 fl oz) of the coconut milk until thick and oily, add the red curry paste and cook, stirring, until fragrant. Add the remaining coconut milk, stirring gently, until boiling. Add the beans and simmer 5 minutes. Add the fish balls and when they come back to a boil, reduce heat and simmer for 3 minutes longer. Shake the pan gently from time to time to prevent sticking. Stir in the spring onions, thick coconut milk, palm sugar and lime juice. Simmer 1 minute more. Garnish with sliced chilli and coriander leaves.

Stuffed fried crab

500 g (1 lb) small mussels

125 g (4 oz) pork mince (ground pork)

2 teaspoons Pepper and Coriander Paste (*page 23*), or Red Curry Paste (*page 20*)

1 tablespoon finely chopped lemon grass

½ teaspoon grated kaffir lime rind

2 tablespoons thinly sliced spring onions

2 teaspoons cornflour (cornstarch)

2 teaspoons fish sauce

1 teaspoon palm sugar

1 egg white

Curry sauce:

1½ cups (12 fl oz) coconut milk

2 tablespoons Green Curry Paste (*page 21*)

2 or 3 kaffir lime leaves

2 tablespoons fish sauce

1 tablespoon lime juice

1 red chilli, sliced

2 spring onions, chopped

Stuffed curried mussels
(Hor Mok Mang Poo)

Filled with a spicy pork mixture and simmered in a curry sauce, these mussels are delicious.
Serves 4

Scrub the mussels well with a brush under cold water. Beard them by giving a sharp tug at the brown fibres protruding from the shell. The shells should be tightly shut – discard any which are not. Place the mussels on a rack and steam just until the shells open. Discard any which remain closed. Remove each top shell and discard.

Combine the pork and the next 8 ingredients, mixing well. Top each mussel with a heaped teaspoon of the mixture, smoothing it neatly into the shell.

Heat about ½ cup of the rich top portion of the coconut milk until oil appears around the edges, add the green curry paste and cook, stirring, for a few minutes until fragrant. Stir in the rest of the coconut milk, add the lime leaves and fish sauce and stir until simmering. On a low heat cook the mussels in this sauce for 10 minutes or until the filling is firm. Add the lime juice, red chilli and spring onions and simmer for a minute longer.

Serve with rice.

Stuffed curried mussels, Hot and sour prawns with cucumber, Prawn balls

750 g (1½ lb) prawns (shrimp)
1 large green cucumber
1½ cups (12 fl oz) coconut milk
2 tablespoons Red Curry Paste (*page 20*)
2 teaspoons dried tamarind pulp
½ cup (4 fl oz) hot water
2 tablespoons fish sauce
1 tablespoon palm sugar
2 or 3 red chillies, finely sliced
1 tablespoon lime juice

Hot and sour prawns with cucumber
(Goong Lon Tang-Gwa)

Serves 6

Shell and devein the prawns. Halve the cucumber and scrape out the seeds. Peel and slice thinly.

Heat about ½ cup (4 fl oz) of the thick top of the coconut milk until oil shows around the edges. Add the red curry paste and stir over medium heat until fragrant. Stir in the remaining coconut milk and bring to a boil. Add the prawns and cucumber, return to the boil and cook for 2 minutes. Soak tamarind pulp in hot water, dissolve and strain. Mix in the tamarind liquid, fish sauce, palm sugar, chillies and lime juice. Serve with rice or noodles.

1 medium or 2 small whole fish
coarse salt
1 teaspoon finely grated fresh ginger
½ teaspoon salt
Sauce:
1 tablespoon peanut oil
1 teaspoon finely chopped garlic
1 tablespoon shredded ginger
4 spring onions (scallions), finely sliced
1 teaspoon palm sugar
1 tablespoon tamarind pulp concentrate, or lime juice
1 tablespoon fish sauce
¼ cup (2 fl oz) water
1 teaspoon cornflour (cornstarch)
fresh coriander (cilantro/Chinese parsley) leaves
red chilli strips

Steamed fish with tamarind and ginger
(Planung Khing)

While there are many recipes for fried fish with tamarind, if you buy a delicate white fish try cooking it in steam rather than oil. The piquant sauce with tamarind makes it a tasty dish.
Serves 4

Have the fish cleaned and scaled. Dip kitchen paper towels in coarse salt and scrub inside the cavity to get rid of any blood. Rinse and blot dry. Score the fish from head to tail three or four times, depending on the size of the fish. Rub inside and out with the grated ginger and ½ teaspoon of salt. Place in a lightly oiled heatproof dish and steam over boiling water until the fish is done, about 10 minutes. The flesh should be opaque when tested at the thickest part. Carefully remove to a plate and keep warm while making the sauce.

Sauce:
Heat the oil and on a low heat fry the garlic for a few seconds, stirring. Add the ginger shreds and spring onions, and cook for a few seconds longer until they are soft. Add sugar, tamarind pulp or lime juice, fish sauce and ¼ cup (2 fl oz) water. Bring to the boil, stir in the cornflour mixed with a tablespoon of cold water, and as soon as it clears and thickens, spoon over the fish. Garnish with fresh coriander and chilli, and serve with steamed long grain (jasmine) rice.

Steamed fish with tamarind and ginger

1 kg (2 lb) fish
1 teaspoon salt
1 teaspoon ground turmeric
½ teaspoon pepper
oil for shallow-frying
1½ teaspoons crushed garlic
2 tablespoons light soy sauce
2 tablespoons fish sauce
¼ cup (2 fl oz) tamarind liquid (page 217)
1 tablespoon palm sugar
1 or 2 fresh red chillies, sliced
3 tablespoons sliced spring onions (scallions)
fresh coriander (cilantro/Chinese parsley)

Fried fish with tamarind sauce
(Pla Jian)

Use this piquant sauce on whole fish, fillets or cutlets. It stands up well to any strongly flavoured fish.

Serves 4

Wash and dry the fish thoroughly and rub over with salt, turmeric and pepper. Heat the oil and fry the fish on medium heat until golden on both sides. Drain on absorbent paper.

Pour away all but 1 tablespoon of oil and fry the garlic over low heat, stirring, until it is pale golden. Add the sauces, tamarind liquid and sugar mixed together. When boiling, add the fish and simmer over medium heat for a few minutes until the sauce is slightly thick. Add the chillies and spring onions, simmer 1 minute more, and serve garnished with coriander leaves.

750 g (1½ lb) large raw prawns (jumbo shrimp)

1 cup (8 fl oz) thick coconut milk

2–3 tablespoons Red Curry Paste (*page 20*)

2 cups (16 fl oz) thin coconut milk

4 kaffir lime leaves

½ teaspoon finely grated lime rind

2 tablespoons fish sauce

2 teaspoons palm sugar

Red curry of prawns
(Kaeng Phed Goong)

For the best flavour, cook and serve the prawns in their shells. If you follow my directions on how to prepare them, it will be easy to remove the shell with spoon and fork.
Serves 6

With kitchen scissors trim each prawn's long feelers and cut open the shell down the curve of the back but do not remove it. With a sharp, pointed knife slit the flesh to expose the vein and lift it out. Rinse and drain the cleaned prawns.

In a wok or frying pan, heat the thick coconut milk until bubbling, add the red curry paste and cook, stirring, until the oil shines on the surface and it smells fragrant. Add the thin coconut milk, lime leaves and rind, fish sauce and palm sugar. Bring to a boil, then add the prawns and simmer uncovered, stirring now and then, for 15 minutes, or until the prawns are cooked and the sauce has slightly reduced and thickened. Serve with rice and a cucumber or cabbage salad.

185 g (6 oz) raw prawn (shrimp) meat

2 spring onions (scallions), finely chopped

1 teaspoon Pepper and Coriander Paste (*page 23*)

1 teaspoon cornflour (cornstarch)

1 teaspoon fish sauce

¼ cup roasted rice powder, or dried breadcrumbs

oil for frying

Fried prawn balls
(Look Chin Goong Tod)

Serve as an accompaniment to rice and curries, or as an appetiser or party savoury.
Makes 12–16

Remove any veins from the prawns. Chop the prawns finely and mix in the rest of the ingredients except the rice powder and oil. Form into small, marble-sized balls and roll in rice powder or breadcrumbs to coat.

Heat the oil in a wok or frying pan and fry a few balls at a time until golden. They will not need long cooking. Drain on absorbent paper and serve warm.

Red curry of prawns

12 crab claws
250 g (8 oz) pork mince (ground pork)
375 g (12 oz) raw prawns (shrimp), shelled, deveined and chopped
1 tablespoon Pepper and Coriander Paste (*page 23*)
1 tablespoon fish sauce
1 or 2 small red chillies, chopped
2 tablespoons finely chopped spring onions (scallions)
Curry Sauce (*page 101*)

Curry of crab claws and prawn balls
(Kaeng Phed Gampoo, Look Chin Goong)

This is a variation on Red Curry of Crab, but easier to eat because you don't have to ferret out the meat from within the crab shells. Ready-shelled claws may be bought, usually by the box, from a good fish shop, stored in the freezer and used as required.
Serves 4–6

Thaw the crab claws. Combine the pork mince with the prawns, pepper and coriander paste, fish sauce, chillies and spring onions. Form into small balls.

Prepare the curry sauce using the same ingredients as in the Red Curry of Crab recipe on *page 101*. When the gravy has simmered for 10 minutes, add the balls and simmer until firm, shaking the pan rather than stirring so they don't break up. Cook for 5 minutes, then add the crab claws, gently slipping them into the sauce so they will absorb as much flavour as possible. Simmer for a further 10–15 minutes, and serve with freshly cooked rice.

12 frozen crab claws
1 teaspoon chopped coriander (cilantro/Chinese parsley) roots
5 whole black peppercorns
1 tablespoon finely chopped lemon grass
150 g (5 oz) raw prawn (shrimp) meat, finely chopped
150 g (5 oz) minced (ground) pork
2 tablespoons finely chopped fresh coriander
½ teaspoon salt

Sauce:

2 tablespoons sweet hot chilli sauce
2 teaspoons fish sauce
2 tablespoons lime juice
2 teaspoons palm sugar, or 1½ tablespoons sugar
4 tablespoons water
2 teaspoons cornflour (cornstarch), or arrowroot

Crab claws with chilli sauce
(Gampoo Yudsai Lard Prik)

Serves 4–6

Thaw the crab claws. Pound the coriander roots, peppercorns and lemon grass to a fine paste. Mix with the prawn meat and pork. Add chopped fresh coriander and salt and mix well. Divide into 12 equal portions and mould around the flesh of the crab claws. Steam over boiling water for 10–12 minutes.

Sauce:
Place all the ingredients except the cornflour in a small pan and cook, stirring, until boiling. Mix the cornflour with a little cold water, stir into the sauce until it thickens and spoon over the crab claws.

Crab claws with chilli sauce

500 g (1 lb) medium-sized raw prawns (shrimp)
2 teaspoons finely chopped fresh ginger
1 tablespoon fish sauce
1 teaspoon sugar
½ cup sliced spring onions
4–6 dried red chillies
2 teaspoons finely chopped fresh or frozen galangal
1 tablespoon chopped lemon grass
½ teaspoon finely grated kaffir lime rind
½ teaspoon black peppercorns
4 cloves garlic
2 coriander (cilantro/Chinese parsley) roots or 6 stalks, chopped
1 small onion, finely chopped
2 tablespoons oil
¾ cup (6 fl oz) thick coconut milk
1 teaspoon rice flour
½ teaspoon salt
fine shreds of fresh lime leaves and fresh chilli

Chilli prawn with shredded lime leaf
(Phat Prik Goong Bai Makrut)

As in other Thai recipes, the lime leaf referred to is kaffir lime, (*citrus hystrix*). While the dried leaves may be simmered in curries and soups, where used as a feature of the dish as in this recipe, they must be fresh. If you haven't a source of fresh kaffir lime leaves, don't despair. I have used other varieties of young citrus leaves from my garden and while they don't have quite the same fragrance, they do add a certain magic to the dish when a shred is bitten into.
Serves 4–6

Shell the prawns, leaving just the last segment of shell and the tail. Devein carefully, and with a sharp knife slit each prawn in half from the top, for about a third of its length. Combine the ginger, fish sauce, sugar and spring onions with the prawns and set aside to marinate for about 10 minutes.

Remove the stalks and shake the seeds out of the dried chillies, and soak the chillies in hot water for 10 minutes. Pound together chillies, galangal, lemon grass, lime rind, peppercorns and garlic, coriander and onion to form a paste.

Heat a wok or frying pan, add the oil and stir fry the pounded ingredients until fragrant. Add the marinated prawns and cook until they change colour, turning them constantly, about 3 minutes. Remove from the heat.

Heat the coconut milk in a small saucepan, reserving 2 tablespoons for mixing with the rice flour and salt. Stir this mixture into the coconut milk as it comes to the boil and stir constantly for a few seconds until it thickens. Pour it immediately into the centre of a serving plate. Place the prawns on the sauce and sprinkle lightly with the lime leaf and fresh chilli.

1 pomfret (or other delicate flat fish), approximately 500 g (1 lb)
1 tablespoon oil
1½ tablespoons Green Curry Paste (*page 21*)
1 teaspoon lime juice
½ cup grated fresh coconut
2 tablespoons finely sliced spring onions (scallions)
2 tablespoons chopped fresh coriander (cilantro/Chinese parsley)
¾ cup (6 fl oz) coconut milk
1 teaspoon fish sauce
1 small green chilli, chopped
cornflour (cornstarch)
oil for frying

Pomfret with coconut
(Pla Lard Kati)

Serves 2

Have the fish cleaned and scaled if necessary. Lightly score the flesh where it is thickest.

Heat the oil and fry the green curry paste, stirring, until it is fragrant. Take 1 teaspoon of the fried paste and mix it with the lime juice and half the grated coconut. Pack into the cavity of the fish. Add the remaining coconut, the spring onions, coriander, coconut milk, fish sauce and green chilli to the fried curry paste and simmer, stirring, for 5 minutes. Cool slightly, then purée in a blender at high speed.

Dust the fish with cornflour to coat. Heat oil for shallow-frying and fry the fish, first on one side and then the other, until golden brown. Transfer to a serving plate and spoon the sauce over to coat. Serve the remaining sauce in a separate bowl.

Red curry of crab

Red curry of crab
(Kaeng Phed Poo)

4 medium or large live crabs

Curry sauce:

2–3 tablespoons Red Curry
Paste (*page 20*)

1 teaspoon finely grated kaffir
lime rind

½ cup chopped small purple
shallots

1 cup (8 fl oz) thick coconut
milk

6 kaffir lime leaves

3 tablespoons finely sliced
lemon grass

2 or 3 green chillies, sliced

2½ cups (20 fl oz) coconut
milk

1 tablespoon fish sauce

1 tablespoon palm sugar

2 tablespoons lime juice

This is such a superb dish that when we eat it at home, it is the only
dish on the menu, served with steaming hot white rice. One needs
to concentrate on picking the sweet flesh from the crabs, and other
dishes would only be a distraction.
Serves 4–6

Either put the crabs in the freezer for several hours, or boil them
just long enough for the shells to turn red — there seems to be no
agreement on which is the more humane method of dispatching
them. Remove the top shells and clean the crabs, discarding the
feathery tissue under the carapace. Break the bodies in halves and
crack the large claws so flavours can penetrate.

Combine the red curry paste with the lime rind (use any
available limes if kaffir limes prove elusive) and the shallots. Heat
the thick coconut milk in a wok or frying pan and cook, stirring,
until oily. Add the curry paste mixture and stir over medium heat
until it smells fragrant.

Add the lime leaves, lemon grass, chillies and the 2½ cups
(20 fl oz) coconut milk. Stir while bringing it to simmering point.
Add the crabs and simmer for 15–20 minutes, or until the crabs are
cooked. Stir in the fish sauce, palm sugar and lime juice and cook a
few minutes longer, adding a little hot water if the sauce has
reduced too much. Serve with white rice.

Poultry

Chicken is commonly found on the menu of the average family, duck more rarely. Poultry in Asian countries are scrawny specimens hanging in unattractive nakedness compared with the plump, politely-packaged birds the Western shopper buys at the supermarket or butcher. It must also be said that these lean birds are fresh, not frozen and while they require longer cooking to become tender, they have more flavour. I think most city dwellers in Western countries have forgotten – if they ever knew – what chicken should taste like.

If you have access to fresh, free-range chickens they are obviously ideal, but all our recipes were tested with readily available supermarket roasting chickens. Cooking the Thai way with clever use of herbs and spices is an ideal way to compensate for lack of flavour in the poultry itself.

½ a roasted duck
½ a pineapple
2 fresh red chillies, or small capsicums (sweet peppers)
1 cup sliced canned bamboo shoot
6 fresh or dried kaffir lime leaves
1 x 400 ml (13 fl oz) can coconut milk, or 2 cups (16 fl oz) fresh coconut milk
1–2 teaspoons Red Curry Paste (*page 20*)
2 tablespoons fish sauce
20 fresh basil leaves
2 teaspoons palm sugar, or brown sugar

Roast duck curry with pineapple

(Kaeng Phed Ped Yang Subparot)

A quick, easy and not-too-hot curry, fragrant with basil and citrus leaves. The reason it uses only half a duck is because rather than go to the trouble of roasting a duck, it may be purchased ready-cooked from an Asian store where they sell just as much or as little as you require.
Serves 4

Chop the duck into pieces through the bone, or remove the bones and cut the meat into bite-sized pieces. Peel and core the pineapple, remove 'eyes' and cut the flesh into bite-sized pieces. Split the chillies and remove the seeds. (Small chillies are very hot, so if a mild flavour is preferred, use large chillies or capsicums.) Cut the bamboo shoot into bite-sized pieces. If using dried lime leaves, soak them in a little hot water. Leave four leaves whole and finely shred the other two, first removing the tough centre rib.

Heat ½ cup (4 fl oz) of the canned coconut milk or the first extract of fresh coconut in a pan, and when bubbling stir in the red curry paste. Fry, stirring, until it becomes oily. Add the pieces of duck and toss with the curry mixture, then add another ½ cup of coconut milk and 1 cup (8 fl oz) of water.

Add the pineapple, chillies, bamboo shoot, the whole lime leaves and fish sauce. Simmer for 10–15 minutes, until the sauce is reduced and thickened. Add the basil leaves and palm sugar, stirring to dissolve the sugar. Finally, stir in the rest of the coconut milk and serve sprinkled with the shredded lime leaves and accompanied by steamed long grain (jasmine) rice (*page 148*).

1 kg (2 lb) chicken half-breasts
1 teaspoon crushed garlic
2 teaspoons finely grated fresh ginger
1 tablespoon Red Curry Paste (*page 20*)
2 tablespoons peanut oil
1 cup spring onions (scallions), cut into 5 cm (2 in) lengths
¼ cup roasted peanuts, crushed, or 2 tablespoons crunchy peanut butter
2 teaspoons palm sugar
1 tablespoon fish sauce
1 cup (8 fl oz) coconut milk
2 cups broccoli florets

Chicken in spicy peanut sauce

(Gai Phad Sauce Tua)

When you have a supply of curry pastes, a dish like this one can be made in less than half an hour.
Serves 6

Cut each half-breast in half again with a sharp chopper, wash them to get rid of any splinters of bone, and dry well on paper towels. Combine the garlic, ginger and red curry paste and rub well over the chicken pieces. Set aside for about 20 minutes.

Heat a wok, pour in the oil and swirl to coat the wok. Toss the spring onions in the oil for a few seconds, remove and set aside. Fry the chicken pieces, turning them over until browned all over. Add the peanuts or peanut butter, palm sugar, fish sauce and coconut milk. Stir well to combine. Cover and simmer until the chicken is tender, and if the sauce reduces too much add a little water and stir well. Meanwhile, blanch the broccoli florets in boiling water for 2 minutes. Drain. Add the broccoli and spring onions to the chicken and mix gently. Serve hot with rice, and a tangy salad.

Chicken in spicy peanut sauce

1.5 kg (3 lb) roasting chicken, or chicken pieces

3 teaspoons chopped garlic

2 teaspoons salt

2 tablespoons black peppercorns

1 cup finely chopped fresh coriander (cilantro/ Chinese parsley), including roots

2 tablespoons lime juice

tomatoes

spring onion (scallion) curls

Barbecue garlic chicken

Barbecued garlic chicken
(Gai Yang)

This versatile recipe may be used with chicken pieces, such as thighs or half-breasts, or a boned half-chicken which makes serving easy — it is simply sliced through, the only bone left being in the wing.
Serves 6

Cut the chicken in half lengthways, and if you like, remove the bones with a small, pointed knife, leaving only the wing bones.

Crush the garlic with the salt to a smooth purée. Coarsely crush the peppercorns in a mortar and pestle or a blender. Combine in a flat dish with the coriander, and the lime juice. Rub the mixture well into the chicken on all sides, cover and refrigerate overnight, or at least 1 hour.

Since a boned chicken does not stay in shape as well as one with the bones in, use poultry skewers to hold it firm and make it easy to turn while cooking. Barbecue over glowing coals, approximately 15 cm (6 in) from the heat. Cook, turning every 5 minutes or so, until the chicken is no longer pink and the skin is crisp. If the weather doesn't permit barbecuing, cook under a preheated griller (broiler).

To serve a boned chicken, place the halves skin side upward on a platter or board and slice with a sharp knife into diagonal slices. If the chicken is not boned, separate into joints. Garnish with tomatoes and curls of spring onion. Serve with a salad of sliced cucumber, spring onions and tomatoes seasoned with lime juice and salt.

500 g (1 lb) chicken thigh fillets

3 or 4 dried chillies

1 small onion

2 teaspoons chopped garlic

1 teaspoon chopped galangal

1 teaspoon chopped lemon grass

1 teaspoon chopped coriander (cilantro/Chinese parsley) root

½ teaspoon kaffir lime rind

1 teaspoon salt

1 teaspoon dried shrimp paste

¼ teaspoon peppercorns

2 tablespoons oil

1 cup (8 fl oz) coconut milk

1 tablespoon fish sauce

1 tablespoon palm sugar

3 kaffir lime leaves

20 fresh sweet basil leaves

Chicken curry
(Kaeng Gai)

This curry doesn't use any of the pastes, but has a special combination of spices which is very individual.
Serves 6

Cut the chicken into bite-sized pieces. Seed and soak the chillies and chop the onion. Pound the chillies and onion to a paste in a mortar and pestle, adding the garlic, galangal, lemon grass, coriander root, lime rind, salt, shrimp paste and peppercorns. Or put into a blender container and grind until smooth, adding 1 tablespoon oil to facilitate blending.

Heat a wok, add 1 tablespoon oil and fry the pounded mixture, stirring constantly, until oil appears on the surface. Add the chicken and stir-fry until it changes colour, then stir in the coconut milk, fish sauce, palm sugar and kaffir lime leaves. Simmer until the chicken is tender. Add the sweet basil leaves and serve with steaming hot rice.

Boned barbecued garlic chicken

300 g (10 oz) chicken thigh fillets
100 g (3½ oz) snow peas (*mange-tout*)
1 cup (8 fl oz) coconut milk
2 tablespoons Green Curry Paste (*page 21*)
1 tablespoon fish sauce
4 kaffir lime leaves
1 or 2 fresh green chillies, sliced
20 sweet basil leaves

Chicken fillet with snow peas
(Kaeng Khiew Wan Gai Tua)
Serves 4

Cut the chicken into bite-sized pieces. String the snow peas and set them aside.

In a wok, heat ½ cup (4 fl oz) coconut milk and when it is bubbling add the green curry paste and stir over medium heat until it smells fragrant. Add the fish sauce and chicken pieces and stir constantly until the chicken is coated with the mixture and is no longer pink.

Mix the remaining ½ cup coconut milk with ½ cup water and add to the pan with kaffir lime leaves and chillies. Simmer gently for 15 minutes, stir in the snow peas and basil leaves and simmer 5 minutes longer. Serve with freshly cooked white rice.

250 g (8 oz) chicken thigh fillets
1 teaspoon crushed garlic
¼ teaspoon whole black peppercorns
½ cup chopped coriander (cilantro/Chinese parsley), including roots
small piece fresh turmeric root, or ½ teaspoon ground turmeric
¼ teaspoon salt
1 teaspoon *Tom Yum* Paste (*page 22*)
2 tablespoons peanut oil
250 g (8 oz) fresh asparagus
100 g (3½ oz) snow peas (*mange-tout*)
¼ cup drained sataw nuts
1 or 2 fresh green chillies
1 tablespoon fish sauce, or to taste
2 cups (16 fl oz) coconut milk
20 sweet basil leaves
2 tablespoons fresh coriander leaves

Chicken and sataw nuts
(Gai Phad Sataw)

This is a dish from southern Thailand where sataw (also spelled 'sator') nuts are very popular. Though called nuts, they are soft, fresh green seeds of a giant bean. They have a distinctive flavour, which could take a little getting used to, and are available bottled in brine, or in cans under the name Petai.
Serves 4–6

Trim every bit of skin and fat from the chicken fillets and cut the meat into very thin shreds. Pound the garlic, peppercorns, coriander and turmeric with a mortar and pestle until it is a paste. Add the salt and *tom yum* paste and marinate the chicken in this mixture for at least 1 hour.

Heat a wok, add the oil and swirl around in the wok. Add the marinated chicken and stir-fry on high heat until the chicken changes colour. Add the asparagus cut into bite-sized pieces, the snow peas, sataw nuts, chillies and fish sauce. Add the coconut milk, stirring constantly. Toss in the basil and coriander leaves and simmer, uncovered, for 5–10 minutes. Serve with steamed rice.

Chicken fillet with snow peas

12 chicken wings
250 g (8 oz) minced (ground) pork
1 teaspoon sugar
2 tablespoons fish sauce
½ cup finely chopped spring onions (scallions)
2 teaspoons Pepper and Coriander Paste (*page 23*)
30 g (1 oz) bean starch noodles, soaked to soften
¾ cup (3 oz) rice flour
oil for frying
Peanut Sauce

Topping and garnish:

¾ cup (6 fl oz) coconut milk
1 teaspoon rice flour
½ teaspoon salt
2 fresh kaffir lime leaves, finely shredded
1 red chilli, finely shredded

1 tablespoon oil
2–3 teaspoons crushed dried chilli flakes
½ cup finely sliced shallots
1 tablespoon Red Curry Paste (*page 20*)
2 kaffir lime leaves
1–1½ cups (8–12 fl oz) coconut milk
¾ cup crunchy peanut butter
2 tablespoons palm sugar
2 tablespoons tamarind liquid
2–3 tablespoons lime juice

Stuffed chicken wings
(Peek Gai Yud Sai)

Not as difficult as it sounds, especially if you buy medium-sized wings. Large wings with well-developed sinews holding the bones in place require more effort – but a small, sharp, pointed knife carefully used is invaluable.
Serves 6–8

Cut the chicken wings at the first joint and keep the top joint for another dish. To remove the two bones in the wing, place the point of a knife between them and run the knife around the top of each bone. Push the flesh down and off the bone and carefully twist each bone out.

Chop the pork to a paste or place in a food processor with the sugar, fish sauce, spring onions, and pepper and coriander paste. Process until smooth, then remove from the processor and mix in the drained bean starch noodles, chopped into short lengths. Fill the boned section of the wings with 1–2 teaspoons of filling in each. Do not overfill or they will burst when steamed. Secure the tops with a small skewer. (Two wings should fit on each skewer.)

Steam over boiling water for 6 or 7 minutes, then leave to cool. Dust with rice flour, deep-fry in hot oil and drain on absorbent paper. Serve with about 1 cup of peanut sauce and coconut topping, garnished with shreds of lime leaf and chilli.

Coconut topping:
Bring the coconut milk, rice flour and salt gently to the boil, stirring, until the coconut milk thickens. Spoon over the chicken wings and peanut sauce.

Peanut sauce
(Nam Jim Tua)

This will make about 2 cups (16 fl oz). Use about 1 cup for the Stuffed Chicken Wings and store the rest in the refrigerator ready to serve on vegetables or with grilled meats like satays.

Heat the oil and carefully fry the dried chilli flakes on low heat. Add the shallots, red curry paste and lime leaves and cook until fragrant. Stir in 1 cup (8 fl oz) coconut milk, the peanut butter, palm sugar and tamarind liquid. Bring to the boil, stirring, and add the lime juice. Thin to a pouring consistency with extra coconut milk or water.

Stuffed chicken wings

500 g (1 lb) shredded duck meat, skin and bones removed
2 cups (16 fl oz) coconut milk
3 kaffir lime leaves
2 tablespoons fish sauce, or to taste
5 large dried chillies
2 teaspoons finely chopped galangal, or 1 teaspoon ground galangal
2 tablespoons finely sliced lemon grass
½ teaspoon finely grated kaffir lime rind
1 tablespoon chopped coriander (cilantro/Chinese parsley) roots
3 teaspoons chopped garlic
½ teaspoon black peppercorns
1 teaspoon dried shrimp paste
2 cups (16 fl oz) thick coconut milk
2 teaspoons palm sugar
3 tablespoons crushed roasted peanuts, or crunchy peanut butter
¼ cup pea-sized eggplants (aubergines), (optional)
½ cup lightly packed basil leaves
1 tablespoon sliced hot red chillies
1 cup lychees (1 x 570 g/ 1 lb 2 oz) can, drained and tossed in a little lime juice and salt
1 tablespoon lime juice
1 teaspoon salt, or to taste
a few shreds of lime leaf

Duck with lychees

Duck Masaman curry

Duck with lychees
(Kaeng Ped Linjee)

Serves 4–6

Simmer the duck in the coconut milk with the lime leaves and fish sauce, until the meat is tender. Remove the seeds from the dried chillies, break the chillies in pieces and pour a little boiling water over. Leave to soak for 10 minutes. Put the drained chillies, galangal, lemon grass, lime rind, coriander roots, garlic, peppercorns and shrimp paste in a mortar and pound to a paste. Alternatively, grind in an electric blender, using a little water from the soaked chillies to facilitate blending.

Set aside ½ cup of the thick coconut milk. Put the rest in a wok or saucepan and bring to the boil, stirring constantly. When thick and oily add the ground ingredients and stir while simmering until thick and fragrant. Add the palm sugar and peanuts or peanut butter and mix well. Stir in the eggplants if used, and the drained duck meat. Continue simmering for 10 minutes, then add the basil leaves. Reserve 1 teaspoon of the sliced chillies and add the remainder to the curry. Cook a couple of minutes longer, adding some of the liquid in which the duck was cooked. When reduced and thickened, stir in the lychees, lime juice and salt. Serve topped with the reserved thick coconut milk and garnished with the remaining sliced chillies and a few shreds of lime leaf. Serve with rice.

8 dressed quail
2 teaspoons Pepper and Coriander Paste (*page 23*)
2 teaspoons Red Curry Paste (*page 20*)
2 teaspoons Sweet Chilli Sauce (*page 84*)
1 teaspoon Golden Mountain sauce (*see* Glossary *page 210*), or light soy sauce
1 tablespoon honey
1 tablespoon peanut oil

Grilled spiced quail

(Nok-Krata Yang)

Serves 4–8

Wash and dry the quail and truss them, holding the legs together with a poultry skewer. Combine the rest of the ingredients and brush over the birds. Marinate for at least an hour. Dry them on paper towels if they become wet, and brush again with the remaining marinade mixture. Grill over glowing coals or under a griller (broiler) at a good distance from the heat so the birds are cooked through. While cooking, brush them with a little oil mixed with the remaining marinade.

500 g (1 lb) chicken thighs
3 cups mixed vegetables such as green beans, asparagus, bamboo shoots, bean sprouts
4 or 5 dried red chillies
½ cup dried shrimp
3 cloves garlic
1½ cups (12 fl oz) thick coconut milk
2 tablespoons palm sugar, or brown sugar
2 tablespoons fish sauce
1 tablespoon lime juice
1 tablespoon tamarind pulp

Topping:

½ cup (4 fl oz) thick coconut milk
½ teaspoon salt
1 teaspoon rice flour
¼ cup crushed toasted peanuts

Chicken and vegetables with chilli- shrimp sauce

(Gai, Pak Phad, Nam Prik)

Steam or poach the chicken until cooked, allow to cool then cut in thick slices, discarding the bones. Blanch each vegetable separately in lightly salted boiling water until tender but still crisp. Refresh in iced water to stop cooking and set the colour, then drain.

Break off the tops of the dried chillies and shake out the seeds. Soak chillies and dried shrimp in hot water for 10 minutes to soften, then drain. Chop the chillies and pound to a paste with the shrimp and garlic in mortar and pestle.

Heat ½ cup (4 fl oz) of the coconut milk until oily and add the pounded mixture. Stir in the palm sugar, fish sauce, lime juice and tamarind. Cook until syrupy and gradually stir in the remaining cup of coconut milk and simmer to reduce. The sauce will darken as it reduces.

Arrange the prepared vegetables on a serving plate, place the sliced chicken on top and pour the sauce over.

Topping:
In a small pan heat the coconut milk, salt and rice flour, stirring, until it thickens. Spoon over the sauce, sprinkle with toasted peanuts and serve at once.

Chilli chicken with noodles

250 g (8 oz) boneless chicken
4 tablespoons peanut oil
2 dried red chillies
1 tablespoon dried garlic flakes
½ cup peanuts
1 tablespoon Red Curry Paste (*page 20*)
¼ (2 fl oz) cup water
2 tablespoons chilli sauce, optional
2 tablespoons fish sauce
220 g (7 oz) rice noodles, cooked and drained
2 tablespoons lime juice
½ cup sliced spring onions (scallions)
½ cup chopped fresh coriander (cilantro/Chinese parsley)

Chilli chicken with noodles
(Kway Teo Phad)

A good example of how a little meat or poultry can go a long way towards flavouring a whole dish of noodles when spiced up with chillies and garlic.
Serves 4

Remove the skin and excess fat from the chicken and cut the meat into strips. Heat the oil, fry the dried chillies on medium heat until they are puffed up and blackened, then remove to absorbent paper. Fry the garlic flakes on low heat for just a few seconds. Lift them out on a large wire strainer as soon as they turn pale golden, as they will continue to cook in their own heat. Drain. Add the peanuts and stir constantly while frying until they are light brown. Lift out and allow to cool on absorbent paper.

Remove the stalks from the chillies, shake out the seeds and chop the chillies into small pieces. Crush the garlic flakes and peanuts. Mix all three together for sprinkling over the dish at the end.

If necessary, add an extra tablespoon of oil to the wok and fry the red curry paste, stirring, for a couple of minutes. Add the chicken and stir-fry on medium-high heat until the colour changes. Add the water, chilli sauce if used, and the fish sauce. Boil for 1 minute, then add the noodles, lime juice and spring onions, and toss over and over in the spicy mixture until heated through. Sprinkle with the peanut mixture and fresh coriander. Extra fish sauce and lime juice mixed with sliced hot chillies may accompany the noodles for real chilli devotees.

4 medium-sized fillets of chicken breast or thigh
¼ cup dried wood fungus
¼ cup finely shredded ginger
2 tablespoons oil
1 white onion, thinly sliced
1 teaspoon finely chopped garlic
1 tablespoon light soy sauce
1 tablespoon fish sauce
1 tablespoon rice vinegar
1 teaspoon palm sugar, or brown sugar
¼ cup chopped spring onions (scallions)
¼ cup chopped fresh coriander (cilantro/Chinese parsley)

Chicken with ginger and wood fungus
(Gai Phad Khing Hed Hung)

When ginger is young the skin is almost transparent and the tips of the rhizome are pink — perfect for using generously in recipes like this one because it is not too pungent. If more mature ginger is all that is available, halve the amount stated and soak it in lightly salted water for 10 minutes, then dry on kitchen paper.
Serves 4

Cut the chicken into dice, discarding any skin or bones. Rinse the wood fungus and soak in hot water for 10 minutes, or until it has swollen to many times the original size. Drain, discard any gritty portions and cut the fungus into bite-sized pieces.

To cut shreds of ginger, rub off the skin if tender enough, or peel thinly with a potato peeler. Cut very thin lengthwise slices, stack a few slices at a time and cut into thin shreds.

Heat the oil and fry the onion until soft and translucent. Add garlic and stir-fry until golden. Add the chicken and ginger, tossing until the chicken changes colour. Stir in the soy sauce, fish sauce, vinegar and sugar. As soon as the liquid boils, turn heat low, cover and simmer for 3 minutes. Do not overcook. Serve sprinkled with spring onions and fresh coriander.

Chiang Mai chicken salad.
Son-in-law eggs,
Chicken with ginger and
wood fungus

1 large chicken breast
2 stalks lemon grass
2 fresh kaffir lime leaves or other tender citrus leaves
1 tablespoon roasted rice powder (*see* Glossary page 215)
½ teaspoon chilli powder, or to taste
2 tablespoons finely sliced spring onions (scallions), including tops
3 tablespoons chopped fresh mint leaves
3 tablespoons chopped fresh coriander (cilantro/Chinese parsley) leaves
2 tablespoons fish sauce
4 tablespoons lime juice
1 or 2 red chillies, seeded and sliced (*see opposite*)
1 teaspoon sugar
lettuce leaves
1 tablespoon finely sliced red onion
extra mint leaves
chilli flower

Chiang Mai chicken salad
(Larb Gai Chiang Mai)

For convenience, use leftover roast chicken in this recipe – or even ready-cooked barbecued chicken.
Serves 4

Grill (broil) the chicken breast until just cooked through, allow to cool and remove the skin and bones. Chop the meat very finely.

Use only the tender white portion of the lemon grass and cut into very thin slices. Reserve half the slices and finely chop the rest. Slice out the mid-ribs from the lime leaves and shred the leaves very finely.

Put the chopped chicken meat in a bowl and mix with the chopped lemon grass and half the shredded lime leaf, the roasted rice powder, chilli powder, spring onions, mint and coriander. Combine the fish sauce and lime juice, pour half of it over the chicken and toss to mix well. Add the sliced chillies and the sugar to the remaining fish sauce and lime juice, stir to dissolve the sugar and serve in a sauce dish alongside the chicken.

Arrange the chicken on lettuce leaves, scatter the reserved sliced lemon grass and the red onion over, and garnish with mint leaves and a chilli flower. Serve at room temperature.

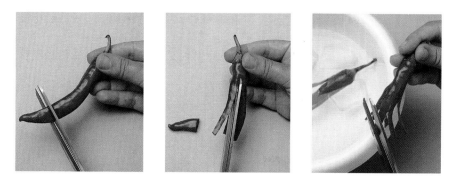

6 eggs
¼ cup (2 fl oz) oil
1 medium onion, sliced thinly
2 fresh chillies, sliced
2 tablespoons palm sugar
3 tablespoons water
2 teaspoons instant tamarind pulp
1 tablespoon fish sauce
chilli flower
coriander (cilantro/Chinese parsley) leaves

Son-in-law eggs
(Kai Look Koei)

Serves 6

Bring the eggs to the boil, stirring gently to centre the yolks. Simmer for 8 minutes, then run cold water into the pan until they are quite cold. Shell the eggs and wipe dry on kitchen paper. Pierce each one 2 or 3 times with a very fine toothpick.

Heat the oil in a wok and fry the eggs until golden and crisp. Drain on absorbent paper. Pour off all but a tablespoon of the oil. Heat it again and stir-fry the onion and chillies until golden and slightly crisp. Drain.

Mix the palm sugar, water, tamarind and fish sauce. Stir over low heat for 5 minutes or until slightly thick. Pour the sauce over the eggs, sprinkle the fried onion and chillies over, and garnish with a chilli flower and coriander leaves. Serve with rice.

250 g (8 oz) chicken fillets, breast or thigh
250 g (8 oz) green beans
1 tablespoon finely sliced lemon grass
2 teaspoons chopped fresh ginger
2 or 3 fresh chillies, seeded and sliced
½ teaspoon grated kaffir lime rind
½ teaspoon black pepper
1 teaspoon garlic, finely chopped
1 tablespoon oil
shredded lettuce or cabbage
¼ cup (2 fl oz) coconut cream
¼ teaspoon salt
1 fresh lime leaf, shredded
extra sliced chillies, (optional)

Chicken with beans
(Gai Phad Tua)

A simple stir-fried combination with the favourite flavours of Thai cuisine.
Serves 4

Slice the chicken into bite-sized strips. Top and tail the beans, cut into 5 cm (2 in) lengths and blanch in boiling water until just tender, drain and refresh in iced water.

In a mortar and pestle pound the lemon grass, ginger, chillies, lime rind, pepper and garlic to a paste. Mix with the chicken, cover and set aside for 10–15 minutes.

Heat the oil in a wok and stir-fry the chicken on medium-high heat until the colour changes, about 3 or 4 minutes. Add the beans and stir-fry for a further minute or two until heated through. Serve on a bed of shredded lettuce or tender cabbage. Heat the coconut cream and salt and spoon over the chicken. Garnish with shreds of lime leaf and extra sliced chillies if desired.

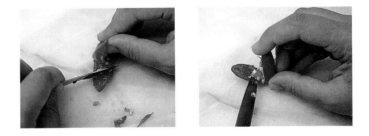

300 g (10 oz) chicken breast
1 piece canned bamboo shoot
½ cup (4 fl oz) thick coconut milk
1½ tablespoons Red Curry Paste (*page 20*)
1 tablespoon finely sliced lemon grass
2 kaffir lime leaves, fresh, frozen or dried
1 cup (8 fl oz) thin coconut milk
2 or 3 fresh red chillies, sliced
1 tablespoon fish sauce
1 tablespoon palm sugar
20 fresh basil leaves
½ cup sliced spring onions (scallions)

Chicken and bamboo shoot curry
(Kaeng Phed Gai Nor Mai)

Serves 4

Remove the skin and bones from the chicken and cut the breast meat into strips. Slice the bamboo shoot thinly, then divide into bite-sized pieces.

Heat the thick coconut milk in a wok and cook the red curry paste, stirring, until fragrant. Add the sliced chicken, lemon grass and lime leaves and cook for 2 or 3 minutes, stirring to coat the chicken with the mixture. Add the thin coconut milk and bamboo shoot and simmer, uncovered, for about 7 minutes. Stir in all the remaining ingredients and cook for 1 minute longer.

Serve hot with rice or noodles.

1 whole chicken breast, steamed

3 cups mixed vegetables

Sauce:

4 or 5 dried chillies

½ cup dried shrimp

2 whole heads pickled garlic

2 tablespoons sesame seeds

4 tablespoons desiccated coconut

¾ cup (6 fl oz) thick coconut milk

2 tablespoons palm sugar

2 tablespoons fish sauce

1 tablespoon lime juice

1 tablespoon dried tamarind, soaked in ½ cup (4 fl oz) hot water and strained (*page 217*)

1 tablespoon crisp fried shallots

Topping:

½ cup (4 fl oz) thick coconut milk

1 teaspoon rice flour

½ teaspoon salt

Chicken salad with vegetables
(Yum Tha Wai)

An easy dish to prepare, ideal to do ahead.
Serves 4–6

Slice the chicken breast into strips. Blanch the vegetables until just half cooked, then drain and refresh in iced water for a few minutes to stop the cooking. Drain again. Arrange the vegetables on a platter and place the chicken strips on top. Prepare the sauce and coconut topping, and just before serving spoon on first the sauce and finally the topping. Sprinkle with the fried shallots, and the reserved toasted coconut and sesame seeds.

Sauce:
Discard the stalks and seeds and break the dried chillies into pieces. Soak in a little boiling water for 10 minutes until softened. Soak the dried shrimp too in just enough hot water to cover, for 10 minutes. Chop the pickled garlic.

Toast the coconut in a dry pan, stirring frequently until golden brown. Turn onto a plate. Wipe out the pan with kitchen paper and toast the sesame seeds too until golden, stirring or shaking the pan so they don't burn. As soon as they are golden, turn out on a plate. Reserve a tablespoon of each for the garnish, and crush the remainder in a mortar and pestle or put into the container of an electric blender. Add the drained chillies, shrimp and pickled garlic and grind everything finely, adding a little coconut milk if necessary to facilitate blending.

Heat the ¾ cup (6 fl oz) thick coconut milk until oily and add the blended mixture. Cook for a few minutes, stirring well. Stir in the palm sugar, fish sauce, lime juice and tamarind liquid. Simmer to reduce and thicken the sauce, and spoon over the chicken and vegetables.

Topping:
In another pan, heat the ½ cup (4 fl oz) thick coconut milk, rice flour and salt, stirring, until it boils and thickens. Gently spoon over the first sauce and sprinkle with the crisp-fried shallots and the reserved toasted coconut and sesame seeds.

Chicken salad with vegetables

250 g (8 oz) chicken breast
6 dried *shiitake* mushrooms
75 g (2½ oz) bean starch noodles
2 coriander (cilantro/Chinese parsley) roots, or 6 stalks, chopped
2 teaspoons chopped garlic
3 red or yellow chillies, sliced
¼ cup spring onions (scallions), chopped
1 litre (4 cups) chicken stock
¼ cup spring onions cut into 4 cm (1½ in) lengths
1 cup young corn cobs, cut into bite-sized pieces
½ cup sliced water chestnuts
½ cup finely sliced bamboo shoot
fresh coriander leaves

Chicken and vegetable soup
(Kaeng Chud Gai Pak)

A satisfying soup, and if the chillies are omitted it is quite mild in flavour.
Serves 6

Remove the skin of the chicken breast and slice the meat thinly. Pour 1 cup (8 fl oz) hot water over the mushrooms in a bowl and leave to soak for 30 minutes. Drain, reserving the soaking water. Discard the stems and slice the caps. Soak noodles in hot water for 15 minutes, drain and cut into short lengths.

Pound the coriander roots, garlic, chillies and the chopped spring onions to a paste and mix with the chicken. Leave to marinate for 10 minutes.

Heat the stock, add the mushrooms and simmer for 5 minutes. Add the next 4 ingredients and simmer for a further 5 minutes. Garnish with coriander leaves.

250 g (8 oz) chicken breast fillets
1 tablespoon oil
1½ teaspoons finely chopped garlic
1 tablespoon shredded fresh ginger
½ cup shredded bamboo shoot
4 fresh red chillies, seeded and finely sliced
1 tablespoon fish sauce
1 tablespoon Golden Mountain sauce (*see* Glossary *page 210*), or oyster sauce
1 teaspoon sugar
4 spring onions (scallions), sliced
½ cup sweet basil leaves

Fried chicken with basil
(Phad Gai Bai Kraprao)

Serves 4

With a sharp knife cut the chicken into thin strips. Heat the oil in a wok and fry the garlic and ginger until golden. Add the chicken and stir-fry 3 or 4 minutes. Add the bamboo shoot, chillies, the sauces, sugar and spring onions. Simmer 3 minutes longer, stir in the basil leaves and serve with rice or noodles.

250 g (8 oz) chicken thigh fillets
1 cup straw mushrooms
2 tablespoons oil
3 tablespoons finely chopped spring onions (scallions)
½ teaspoon finely chopped garlic
1 tablespoon Red Curry Paste (*page 20*)
2 fresh red chillies, seeded and chopped
1 tablespoon fish sauce
½ cup (4 fl oz) thick coconut milk
2 fresh kaffir lime leaves

Chicken and straw mushroom curry

(Phad Phed Gai Hed Farng)

Serves 4

Cut the chicken fillets into dice. If fresh straw mushrooms are used, trim each base, cut the mushrooms in halves from top to bottom and blanch them in boiling water for 1 minute. Drain. If using canned straw mushrooms, drain the liquid away and cut the mushrooms in halves.

Heat a wok, add the oil and when it is hot stir in the spring onions, garlic, red curry paste and chillies. Cook, stirring, for 2 minutes or until fragrant. Add the diced chicken and stir-fry until the colour changes. Stir in the mushrooms, fish sauce and coconut milk, and cook a few minutes longer, uncovered, on medium-low heat. With a sharp knife trim away the tough centre ribs of the lime leaves and shred the leaves finely. Serve the chicken and mushrooms sprinkled with shreds of lime leaves and accompanied by white rice.

1 kg (2 lb) duck
1 cup (8 fl oz) thick coconut milk
3 tablespoons Masaman Curry Paste (*page 21*)
1 cup (8 fl oz) thin coconut milk
3 kaffir lime leaves
1 tablespoon palm sugar
5 cardamom pods, bruised
1 cup pea-sized eggplants (aubergines), optional
2 tablespoons ground roasted peanuts, or crunchy peanut butter
2 tablespoons fish sauce
2 tablespoons tamarind liquid
1 tablespoon lime juice

Duck masaman curry

(Masaman Ped)

This is a Muslim style of curry, featuring the fragrant spices which denote an Indian influence, but somehow tempered with the special flavours of Thailand — a true hybrid.

Serves 4

Cut the duck into serving pieces. Heat ½ cup (4 fl oz) of the thick coconut milk until oily and stir in the Masaman curry paste. Cook, stirring constantly, until fragrant. Stir in the duck pieces, thin coconut milk, lime leaves, palm sugar and cardamom pods. Simmer 30–45 minutes, or until almost tender.

Stir in the eggplants, peanuts or peanut butter and the remaining ½ cup thick coconut milk and cook for 10 minutes longer. Add the fish sauce, tamarind liquid and lime juice. The sauce should be slightly reduced. Garnish and serve with rice.

Meat

The newcomer to Thai food may take one look at the recipes in this chapter and think I'm skimping on portions — but in Thailand, meat is never eaten in large amounts . It is cooked with marvellous flavours of herbs and spices, often has a rich coconut milk sauce, and a little meat is eaten with a large amount of rice. Rice is always the mainstay of the meal.

Don't be surprised to find in certain recipes that meat is combined with seafood, for instance in the Pork and Crab Sausage — it may sound strange, but is quite delicious.

500 g (1 lb) lean stewing beef

½ teaspoon salt

4 cardamom pods, bruised

2½ cups (20 fl oz) thin
coconut milk

2 cups (16 fl oz) thick
coconut milk

2 or 3 tablespoons Masaman
Curry Paste (*page 21*)

10 small new potatoes,
scrubbed

10 pickling onions, peeled

1 tablespoon fish sauce

3 tablespoons lime juice

2 teaspoons palm sugar

15–20 basil leaves

2 tablespoons crushed roasted
peanuts, optional

Masaman beef curry
(Kaeng Masaman Nuer)

In this curry, you will taste the fragrant spices usually associated
with Indian curries.
Serves 4

Cut the beef into large cubes and put into a saucepan with the salt,
cardamom pods and thin coconut milk. Simmer, uncovered, until
the meat is almost tender.

Heat 1 cup (8 fl oz) of the thick coconut milk until oily, stir in
the curry paste and fry, stirring, until it smells fragrant. Stir in the
potatoes, onions and the meat, lifted from its cooking liquid with a
slotted spoon. Reserve the stock for a soup.

Simmer the meat and vegetables until tender, adding the
remaining thick coconut milk as necessary. Stir in the fish sauce,
lime juice, palm sugar and basil leaves. If preferred, sprinkle the
curry with crushed peanuts before serving.

1 kg (2 lb) pork loin

½ cup palm sugar, or brown
sugar

½ cup (4 fl oz) fish sauce

Sweet pork
(Moo Wan)

Pork cooked until tender in a mixture of salty fish sauce and sweet
palm sugar has a quite extraordinary flavour. The skin is shredded
into fine, thread-like strips and included in salads, giving them
another dimension in texture. The meat is cut up and fried in other
dishes such as rice and noodles, but can also be sliced thinly and
served, with chilli sauce, as an accompaniment to rice.
Serves 6–8

Remove the rind from the pork and reserve. The pork may be cut
into pieces or cooked whole, whichever you prefer.

Put the pork and rind into a saucepan with cold water to
cover. Add the sugar and fish sauce, bring to the boil and skim the
top. Turn heat low and simmer, covered, for about 1 hour. Uncover
and continue to cook until the pork is tender and the fat transparent.
The rind too should be soft enough to be pierced easily. Allow to
cool in the liquid.

Masaman beef curry

500 g (1 lb) lean pork
1 tablespoon oil
3 tablespoons Red Curry Paste (*page 20*)
1½ cups (12 fl oz) coconut milk
½ teaspoon grated kaffir lime rind
2 or 3 kaffir lime leaves
2 tablespoons fish sauce
10 fresh basil leaves
1 or 2 red chillies, sliced
1 x 425 g can young corn cobs, drained
3 or 4 fresh kaffir lime or citrus leaves
sliced red chillies

Red pork curry with young corn
(Kaeng Phed Moo Kao Poad Orn)

Serves 4–6

Trim the pork and cut into dice. Heat the oil and fry the curry paste until fragrant. Add the pork pieces and stir-fry until the colour changes. Stir in the coconut milk, lime rind and leaves. Stir until boiling. Reduce heat and simmer for 35 minutes or until the pork is tender, stirring occasionally and adding extra coconut milk if necessary.

When the pork is very tender, stir in the fish sauce, basil leaves, chillies and corn and cook a further 5 minutes. Serve with steamed rice and garnish with shredded kaffir lime leaves and extra sliced chillies.

2 tablespoons oil
1 tablespoon Pepper and Coriander Paste (*page 23*)
1 teaspoon finely chopped garlic
300 g (10 oz) pork and veal mince
1 teaspoon hot chilli sauce
1 teaspoon fish sauce
1 small onion, finely sliced
1 stem lemon grass, finely sliced

Spicy pork mince
(Phad Moo Sub)

This must be one of the quickest and tastiest ways with mince. In Thailand, pork mince (ground pork) would be used, but because most supermarkets and butchers sell a mixture of pork and veal mince, we have used this instead. The results are just as good.
Serves 4–6

Heat a wok, add the oil and swirl to coat. Add the pepper and coriander paste and the garlic and fry, stirring constantly, until fragrant. Add the pork and veal mince and continue to stir, breaking up any lumps, until the meat is no longer pink. Mix in the chilli sauce and fish sauce. Cover with a lid, lower heat and let it simmer for 15 minutes.

Stir in the onion and lemon grass and cook uncovered, stirring frequently, until the liquid reduces almost completely. Serve with rice and a vegetable.

Red pork curry with young corn

Decoration for satay sticks as shown on page 125

¼ cup raw cashews
½ cup (4 fl oz) oil for frying
6 dried red chillies
500 g (1 lb) lean pork, sliced thinly
2 teaspoons Red Curry Paste (*page 20*), or *Tom Yum* Paste (*page 22*)
2 tablespoons fish sauce
2 tablespoons lime juice
1 teaspoon palm sugar
½ cup (4 fl oz) water
2 teaspoons Golden Mountain sauce (*see* Glossary *page 210*)
1 teaspoon cornflour (cornstarch)
lettuce, carrot, cucumber, and lime wedges

Stir-fried chilli pork with cashews
(Moo Phad Mamuang Mimaparn)

A quick dish to make with ready-to-use curry paste, hopefully some you have made and stored in your refrigerator or freezer.
Serves 4

Fry the cashews in the oil over medium heat, stirring constantly, until golden brown. Lift out on a slotted spoon and drain on kitchen paper. Fry the dried chillies just until they turn dark and drain them also. Pour off all but 2 tablespoons of the oil.

On high heat fry the pork until it changes colour. Add the curry paste (or, for a more lemony flavour, use *tom yum* paste) and fry for a few minutes longer. Add the fish sauce, lime juice, sugar and water and simmer for 10 minutes. Add the Golden Mountain sauce to taste. Thicken the sauce with cornflour mixed with a little cold water and turn off the heat before adding in the fried cashews and chillies.

Serve garnished with lettuce, slices of carrot and cucumber, and wedges of lime.

500 g (8 oz) boneless chicken, beef or pork
2 tablespoons oil
1 tablespoon finely sliced lemon grass
1 red chilli, seeded
2 teaspoons chopped garlic
1 teaspoon palm sugar
2 teaspoons fish sauce
bamboo skewers

Mixed satay

Some of the nicest satays I have tasted were at a little family-run noodle shop in Chiang Mai. They were distinctly sweet, and the lady making them said they were marinated only briefly.
The skewers on which the satays are grilled should be soaked in water overnight or for at least 2 hours to prevent them burning.
Serves 4–6

Trim the meat of any excess fat and remove chicken skin. Slice the meat and cut into 5 cm (2 in) long strips. In an electric blender combine the oil, lemon grass, chilli, garlic, palm sugar and fish sauce on high speed to make a purée. Pour over the meat and mix well. Marinate for at least 2 hours.

Thread 2 or 3 pieces of marinated meat onto each skewer and grill (broil) on the barbecue or cook under a preheated griller (broiler), turning 2 or 3 times. The meat should be well done but do not overcook it. Serve with Peanut Sauce (*page 111*) and Cucumber Salad (*page 39*).

Fried chilli pork with cashews

500 g (1 lb) lean grilling steak or premium quality minced steak
4 tablespoons lime juice
2 dried red chillies
3 tablespoons peanut oil
2 tablespoons roasted rice powder
2 stems tender lemon grass or finely grated rind of 1 lemon
½ cup finely chopped purple onion or spring onion
½ cup chopped fresh mint leaves
2 tablespoons fish sauce, or to taste

Garnish:

lettuce leaves
mint sprigs
lime wedges
fresh chilli slices

Minced beef salad

(Larb)

There are two versions of Larb, one based on raw beef like Steak Tartare, while the other is lightly poached. Those who are not brave enough for raw steak may prefer the cooked version. If you wish to try the original, make sure the steak is very fresh, very lean and very finely minced.

Serves 4–6

Ask the butcher to mince the steak for you. Mix in a bowl with the lime juice. Fry the dried chillies in hot oil until they are almost black, about 2 minutes and drain on absorbent paper. When cool they will be crisp and easy to chop finely, almost to a powder. Mix with the roasted rice powder.

Combine all the ingredients thoroughly, then arrange on lettuce leaves and garnish with extra mint sprigs, lime wedges and fresh chilli slices.

For the cooked version, poach the minced beef for a minute or two, only until the colour changes, in a small amount of boiling water. Drain, (save the liquid for soup or curry), mix in all the ingredients, garnish and serve.

Note:

If you cannot find ready roasted and ground rice powder, it is worth making some – the flavour is essential to Larb. In a dry pan over medium heat put 3 tablespoons raw rice and shake the pan or stir constantly until the rice grains are toast brown. Pound in a mortar and pestle.

500 g (1 lb) round or blade steak
1 cup (8 fl oz) thick coconut milk
2–3 tablespoons Panang Curry Paste (*page 23*)
2 cups (16 fl oz) thin coconut milk
2 tablespoons fish sauce
4 fresh or dried kaffir lime leaves
2 red chillies, sliced
2 teaspoons palm sugar
2 tablespoons lime juice
½ cup roasted peanuts
¼ cup chopped fresh coriander
a few fresh basil leaves (optional)

Beef Panang curry

(Panang nuer)

Serves 4

Trim off any fat or sinew and cut the beef into slices, then into bite-sized pieces. Heat half the thick coconut milk in a wok or saucepan and when it is oily, fry the Panang curry paste over medium heat, stirring, until it is fragrant. Add the thin coconut milk, fish sauce, beef, lime leaves and chillies. Simmer until the beef is tender, adding more thin coconut milk if necessary.

Stir in the remaining thick coconut milk, the palm sugar, lime juice and peanuts. Sprinkle with the fresh coriander and basil leaves and serve with rice.

750 g (1½ lb) lean round or blade steak
2 tablespoons peanut oil
3 tablespoons Green Curry Paste (*page 21*)
3 cups (24 fl oz) coconut milk
4 fresh, frozen or dried kaffir lime leaves
2 tablespoons fish sauce
2 fresh green chillies, finely chopped
1 teaspoon palm sugar or brown sugar
¼ cup chopped fresh coriander
¼ cup chopped fresh basil

Green curry of beef
(Kaeng Khiew wan nuer)

Like all curried dishes, this one gets better after a few days in the refrigerator. The recipe may successfully be doubled.
Serves 4–6

Cut the beef into thick strips. Heat the oil and fry the green curry paste over medium heat until it is fragrant. Add the beef and stir fry until it changes colour.

Add the coconut milk and stir until it comes to the boil, then lower heat so it simmers. Add the lime leaves, fish sauce and chillies and cook uncovered over low heat for about 20 minutes, until the beef is tender. Just before serving, stir in the sugar, coriander and basil. Serve with steamed white rice.

1 bunch spinach, about 500 g (1 lb)
500 g (1 lb) lean round steak
4 cups (32 fl oz) coconut milk
3 tablespoons Pepper and Coriander Paste (*page 23*)
2 stems tender lemon grass, finely sliced
1 tablespoon sliced fresh galangal or 3 slices frozen or dried galangal
2 tablespoons fish sauce
1 tablespoon palm sugar or brown sugar

Beef and spinach in coconut milk
(Kaeng nuer gub pak kom)
Serves 6

Wash the spinach well and use only the leaves for this dish. Cut the leaves across twice. Cut the beef into thin strips.

In a wok stir the coconut milk and pepper and coriander paste, lemon grass, galangal, fish sauce and sugar until simmering. Add the beef and cook gently, uncovered, for 20 minutes or until the beef is almost tender. Add the spinach and cook for about 8 minutes. Serve with rice.

½ cup dried shrimp
2 tablespoons peanut oil
1 onion, finely chopped
2 tablespoons Pepper and Coriander Paste (*page 23*)
500 g (1 lb) minced steak
2 teaspoons palm sugar
2–3 tablespoons fish sauce
2 red chillies, seeded and sliced
3 tablespoons soaked wood fungus, sliced
¼ cup fresh mint leaves
¼ cup fresh basil leaves

Minced beef with dried shrimp
(Phad nuer sub goong haeng)
Serves 4–6

Soak the shrimp in hot water for 10 minutes or until softened. Heat the oil in a wok and fry the onion, stirring frequently, until soft and golden. Add the pepper and coriander paste and fry, stirring, for 3 minutes or until fragrant. Add the minced steak and the drained prawns and stir fry until the beef is no longer pink.

Cover and simmer until the liquid that comes out of the beef is almost all absorbed and the beef is tender. Stir in the palm sugar, fish sauce, chillies and wood fungus. Add the fresh mint and basil leaves (which should be roughly chopped if large) and toss together for a minute or two before serving with steamed rice. When served cold it makes a nice addition to a mixed salad.

sausage casing

250 g (8 oz) minced (ground) pork

125 g (4 oz) crab meat

1 tablespoon Red Curry Paste (*page 20*)

¼ cup roasted peanuts, coarsely chopped

¼ cup finely chopped purple shallots, or spring onions (scallions)

2 tablespoons finely chopped fresh coriander (cilantro/ Chinese parsley)

2 teaspoons fish sauce

3 tablespoons thick coconut milk

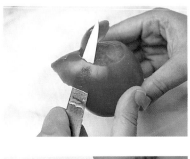

Pork and crab sausage
(Sai Klok Moo Gub Poo)

There are different types of sausages made and sold in Thailand, and, depending on which region the recipe originated in, they are either sour or hot or sweet . . . not totally, but those flavours predominate. Because the traditional way of cooking these sausages is over coals, they are ideal for barbecuing. When the sausage is nearly done, a handful of coconut from which the milk has been extracted is sprinkled over the fire to make fragrant smoke. Remember that when grating fresh coconut, not a bit of it is wasted. The shells make good firewood, and even after extracting three lots of milk, the used flesh can be packed into freezer bags and saved for the day when you want to sprinkle some over hot coals to give your Thai sausages that authentic flavour!
Serves 6

Soak the sausage casing in a sink of cold water while making the filling. The reason I don't give a weight or measurement for this is because you are more or less at your butcher's mercy as you plead with him to part with some of his stock. He will grudgingly give you some and charge you whatever he thinks fit, but put up with it – the sausages are worth it! There are thin and thick sausage casings; we used thin ones, but this is up to you.

Mix all the ingredients for the filling together thoroughly, first making sure there are no bony bits in the crab meat.

Stretch one end of the sausage casing over the cold water tap and run water through. (It may be necessary to trim off any sections through which water spurts, otherwise the sausages will burst when they are filled.)

If you have an efficient sausage-making machine, this is a whole lot easier, but I have done it both ways – with and without. Don't embark on the latter unless you are a very patient person (or a very determined one). Fill the sausage skin and coil it around as in the photograph . Grill (broil) over glowing coals or under a preheated griller (broiler), placing the sausage as far away from the heat as possible so that it cooks thoroughly. Cooking time should be at least 25 minutes. Sprinkle grated coconut on the coals during the last 10 minutes, or use soaked wood chips to impart a different flavour – hickory and mesquite are two of my favourites. Turn the sausage once during grilling.

Slice thickly and serve with rice.

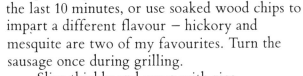

Pork and crab sausages

2 teaspoons finely chopped garlic
½ teaspoon salt
125 g (4 oz) minced (ground) beef
125 g (4 oz) minced (ground) pork
¼ teaspoon ground black pepper
½ teaspoon grated nutmeg
2 tablespoons finely chopped fresh coriander (cilantro/Chinese parsley)
2 tablespoons finely chopped spring onions (scallions)
2 teaspoons fish sauce
1 tablespoon beaten egg
plain (all-purpose) flour
oil for frying

Fried meat balls
(Moo, Nuer Tod Mun)

Serve these as an accompaniment to rice and curry, or simmer them in a curry sauce. The mixture may also be used to fill sections of cucumber or zucchini (courgettes) which are simmered in soups.
Makes about 30 small balls

Sprinkle the garlic with the salt and crush to a smooth purée. Combine the garlic, beef and pork in a bowl with all the other ingredients except the flour and oil. Mix very well to distribute the flavours.

Take teaspoonfuls of the mixture and roll between wet hands to make small balls the size of marbles. Roll in flour and fry in the hot oil over medium-low heat, shaking the pan frequently, until they are golden brown and cooked through. Drain on absorbent paper.

500 g corned (salted) silverside
3 tablespoons oil
1 teaspoon crushed garlic
1 teaspoon chilli powder
1 tablespoon palm sugar
1 tablespoon fish sauce
crisp-fried onion and garlic flakes (*see* Glossary *page 209*), (optional)

Sweet and hot crisp beef
(Nuer Khem Phad)

This side dish served with Iced Rice (*page 150*) is just as delicious with hot rice. The oil in which it is fried is full of flavour and, sparingly mixed with plain steamed rice, makes it delicious.
Serves 4–6

Put the corned beef in a saucepan with cold water to cover and bring to the boil. Turn heat low and simmer, covered, for 1 hour or until the beef is very tender. Drain well, leave until cool enough to handle, then lift it onto a board and gently tease the fibres loose with a fork. Discard any fat or gristle.

Heat the oil in a wok and fry the beef, stirring constantly, for 3 or 4 minutes, or until it is slightly brown and crisp. Add the garlic and chilli powder, and continue tossing for a further minute or until the garlic smells fragrant. Stir in the palm sugar and fish sauce. As the palm sugar melts it will coat the beef. Pour the beef and the oil, flavoured with garlic and chilli, into a serving dish.

Note:
If preferred, sprinkle the beef with crisp-fried onion and garlic flakes.

Pork curry with ginger and pickled garlic

(Moo Phad Khing Kratiem Dong)

A robust-flavoured dish for those who don't flinch from garlic at full strength.
Serves 4–6

750 g (1½ lb) loin of pork

½ cup finely shredded fresh ginger

1 tablespoon sliced fresh garlic

1 onion, chopped

2 tablespoons Red Curry Paste (*page 20*)

1 teaspoon ground turmeric

1 teaspoon finely grated kaffir lime rind

3 tablespoons peanut oil

2 tablespoons fish sauce

5 fresh or dried kaffir lime leaves

1 tablespoon dried tamarind pulp

2 tablespoons sliced pickled garlic

2 teaspoons palm sugar

Cut the pork into 5 cm (2 in) squares. Put half the shredded ginger into a small bowl of salted water and leave to soak. Put the remaining ginger, all the fresh garlic and the onion into a mortar and pestle and pound, or into a blender container and whiz to a smooth purée. Mix with the curry paste, turmeric and kaffir lime rind. Marinate the pork in this mixture for about 20 minutes.

Heat a wok or saucepan and pour in the oil. When the oil is hot fry the pork, stirring, until the colour changes. Add the fish sauce, lime leaves, and the reserved ginger shreds drained from the soaking water. Dissolve the tamarind pulp in 1 cup (8 fl oz) of hot water, strain and add, stirring well. Cover and simmer until the pork is tender. Stir in the pickled garlic and palm sugar, simmer a minute or two longer and serve hot with rice and accompaniments.

Note:
This curry is even nicer when prepared a couple of days before serving. Cool, cover tightly and store in the refrigerator.

Eggs filled with pork and seafood

(Kai Jah)

4 eggs

½ cup chopped raw prawns

½ cup flaked cooked crab meat

½ cup chopped cooked pork

1 teaspoon Pepper and Coriander Paste (*page 23*)

1 tablespoon fish sauce, or ½ teaspoon salt

1–2 tablespoons thick coconut milk

oil for deep-frying

Batter:

½ cup (2 oz) plain (all-purpose) flour

2 tablespoons ground rice

½ cup (4 fl oz) lukewarm water

2 teaspoons oil

Have the eggs at room temperature, not straight out of the refrigerator. Put them into a pan of cold water and slowly bring to the boil, stirring gently for the first 3 minutes so that the yolks are centred. Simmer for 8–10 minutes, then run cold water into the pan to cool the eggs quickly. Remove shells and cut the eggs in halves lengthways.

Scoop out the yolks and mash them with a fork. Add the prawns, crab meat and pork, pepper and coriander paste, fish sauce or salt, and just enough coconut milk to moisten. Mix well. Divide the mixture into 8 equal portions and fill the egg whites, mounding and smoothing the filling to look like a complete egg. Dip in the batter and fry in deep hot oil until golden brown. Drain on absorbent paper and serve warm or cold, with Chilli Sauce (*page 85*) or Peanut Sauce (*page 111*) for dipping.

Batter:
Whisk all the ingredients together until smooth, adding a little extra water if batter is too thick.

3 medium-sized bitter gourds

2 cups (16 fl oz) water

2 tablespoons sugar

Pork Filling:

250 g (8 oz) minced (ground)
   pork

1 teaspoon sugar

1 teaspoon finely grated fresh
   ginger

1 teaspoon crushed garlic

1 tablespoon finely chopped
   spring onions (scallions)

1 tablespoon finely chopped
   fresh coriander
   (cilantro/Chinese parsley)

1 teaspoon Green Curry Paste
   (*page 21*)

1 tablespoon fish sauce

Gravy:

3 tablespoons oil

2 tablespoons Green Curry
   Paste (*see above*)

1 cup (8 fl oz) coconut milk

1 cup (8 fl oz) water

1 teaspoon palm sugar

2 tablespoons fish sauce

3 kaffir lime leaves

Pork with bitter gourd
(Khiew Wan Mara Yud Sai Moo)

Undoubtedly, bitter gourd, or bitter melon as it is sometimes called,
is an acquired taste. Those who have grown accustomed to it relish
it immensely, and eat it fried, cooked in coconut milk, or even raw
as a salad. My favourite way is thinly sliced, sprinkled with salt and
turmeric and left for an hour, then wiped over and shallow-fried
until golden brown.

Choose slender, deep green gourds. Those which are turning
yellow and are too plump indicate over ripeness.

Serves 6

Cut the bitter gourds into 2.5 cm (1 in) slices, discarding the tips and
stem ends. With a small knife hollow out the centre membrane and
seeds. Bring the water and sugar to the boil and blanch the slices, a
few at a time, for 1–2 minutes. Drain.

Mix together all the ingredients for the filling and fill the
gourd slices, packing the pork mixture in firmly. Heat the oil and
fry the gourd, a few slices at a time, to seal the pork and brown it
slightly. Remove to a plate with a slotted spoon and pour off the oil,
leaving only a tablespoon in the pan.

Fry the green curry paste, stirring, until it smells fragrant. Add
the coconut milk, water, palm sugar, fish sauce and lime leaves, and
stir until simmering. Gently slip the bitter gourd slices into the
sauce and simmer for 20 minutes, or until the pork is cooked
through. Serve with rice.

---

500 g (1 lb) belly pork

1 tablespoon fish sauce

1 tablespoon palm sugar

¼ cup pea-sized eggplants
   (aubergines) (optional)

½ cup sliced bamboo shoot

1½ cups (12 fl oz) coconut
   milk

3 tablespoons Panang Curry
   Paste (*page 23*)

15–20 basil leaves

*Steamed rice, Pork Panang
curry, Sweet dipping sauce,
Dried shrimp salad*

Pork Panang curry
(Panang Moo)

Serves 4–6

Cut the belly pork into strips 2 cm (¾ in) wide and 4 cm (1½ in)
long and place in a saucepan with the fish sauce and palm sugar and
just enough water to cover. Simmer until tender and the rind is
clear. Drain and retain the stock.

Meanwhile, blanch and drain the eggplants and slice the
bamboo shoot. Heat half of the coconut milk, add the curry paste
and simmer until fragrant. Stir in the pork and cook until the oil
separates from the gravy. Add the eggplant and bamboo shoot and
simmer for 10 minutes, adding a little pork stock if necessary.
Shortly before serving, stir in the basil leaves. Spoon remaining
coconut milk over and garnish with shreds of red chilli and lime
leaves.

750 g (1½ lb) beef
750 g (1½ lb) pumpkin
2 tablespoons peanut oil
2–3 tablespoons Red Curry Paste (*page 20*)
2 cups (16 fl oz) thin coconut milk
3 kaffir lime leaves
2 or 3 large dried red chillies
5 or 6 fresh red chillies
2 tablespoons fish sauce
1 teaspoon palm sugar
½ cup (4 fl oz) thick coconut milk

Beef and pumpkin curry
(Kaeng Nuer Fug Tong)

The sweetness of pumpkin goes well with the hot flavours of this curry.
Serves 6

Trim off excess fat and cut the beef into cubes. Peel the pumpkin and discard the membrane and seeds from the centre, then cut the pumpkin into cubes of the same size.

Heat the oil in a heavy saucepan or wok and fry the curry paste, stirring over medium heat until it smells cooked and oil shows around the edges. Add the beef cubes and fry them in the mixture, stirring and turning them constantly until they change colour.

Add the thin coconut milk, lime leaves, chillies and fish sauce. Simmer for 30 minutes, then add the pumpkin and stir well. If necessary, add an extra cup (8 fl oz) of coconut milk so there is sufficient liquid to simmer the pumpkin. Continue to cook for a further 35–40 minutes until the pumpkin and beef are tender. Stir in the palm sugar until it dissolves and then the thick coconut milk. Serve the curry with rice.

250 g (8 oz) round steak
2 cups (16 fl oz) coconut milk
2 kaffir lime leaves
2 tablespoons oil
2 tablespoons Red Curry Paste (*page 20*)
2 cups broccoli florets
1 cup young corn cobs
¾ cup (6 fl oz) coconut milk
4 spring onions (scallions), sliced
1 tablespoon fish sauce
1 teaspoon palm sugar
coriander (cilantro/Chinese parsley) leaves

Stir-fried beef with broccoli and corn
(Phad Phed Nuer, Kao Poad Orn)

Serves 4

Slice the beef into strips and cook until tender in the thin coconut milk with the lime leaves. Drain, reserving the liquid.

Heat the oil and cook the red curry paste until fragrant, stirring. Add the beef, broccoli and corn and cook for 3 or 4 minutes, stirring constantly. Add the coconut milk and cook over moderately high heat until it is all absorbed and the meat and vegetables are tender. Add some of the reserved cooking liquid if necessary.

Stir in the spring onions, fish sauce and palm sugar and garnish with coriander leaves. Serve with rice.

1 cup (8 fl oz) coconut milk
3 teaspoons Pepper and Coriander Paste (*page 23*)
500 g (1 lb) lean pork mince
1 stem lemon grass, finely sliced
2 tablespoons Golden Mountain sauce (*see Glossary page 210*)
20 basil leaves
2 red chillies, seeded and sliced

Minced pork with basil
(Moo Sub Bai Kraprao)

Serves 4–6

Heat ½ cup (4 fl oz) coconut milk, add the pepper and coriander paste and cook until it smells fragrant. Stir in the pork mince and lemon grass and simmer until the pork is tender, stirring frequently and adding more coconut milk if required. The meat should be moist, not dry.

A few minutes before serving, stir in the Golden Mountain sauce, basil leaves and red chillies. Serve with steaming hot rice.

250 g (8 oz) rump steak

1 tablespoon Pepper and
Coriander Paste (*page 23*)

2 teaspoons (4 small cloves)
finely chopped garlic

2 tablespoons oil

¼ cup pea-sized eggplants
(aubergines)

½ cup sliced bamboo shoot

½ cup drained straw
mushrooms

2 red chillies, sliced

10 basil leaves

2 teaspoons fish sauce

1 teaspoon palm sugar

2 tender kaffir lime or citrus
leaves, finely shredded

Fried beef with bamboo shoot and mushrooms
(Phad Nuer Normai, Hed)

This is typical of the way a small amount of meat can be stretched
by adding vegetables and sufficiently strong flavours to make the
whole dish tasty.

When not using a whole can of bamboo shoot or straw
mushrooms at one time, these ingredients will keep well in the
refrigerator for about a week, but change the water every day.
Serves 4

Trim off excess fat from the steak and with a sharp knife cut the
meat into thin strips. Marinate with half the pepper and coriander
paste for 1 hour. Fry the garlic in the oil over medium heat, stirring,
for a minute, taking care it does not brown. Add the remaining
pepper and coriander paste and fry for a further minute, or until it
is fragrant. Add the beef and stir-fry until the colour changes and it
is tender.

Add the eggplants, bamboo shoot and the mushrooms, which
may be cut in halves lengthways so they absorb more flavour.
Continue cooking until all the liquid is absorbed. Stir in the chillies,
basil leaves, fish sauce, palm sugar and lime leaves, heat through and
serve with steamed rice or bean starch noodles.

Fried beef with bamboo shoot and mushrooms

Crab fried rice in omelette

Rice and Noodles

Plain white rice, perfectly steamed, is the most important single item in Thai meals. Whatever else is served is termed 'with the rice'. Fried rice with all its additions is a snack eaten on its own – not the central dish in a meal.

Noodles in a host of different sizes are made from rice flour, mung bean starch, wheat flour and eggs. Rice noodles are the most popular in Thailand, and are freshly made each day, but dried rice noodles are perfectly acceptable and have a long shelf life.

Noodles

Noodles are eaten often in Thailand, but they never take the place of rice in a main meal. Mostly, they are the basis of snacks, although there are certain noodle dishes which are quite substantial.

Rice noodles are the most popular variety in Thailand, and there are special noodle shops where fresh rice noodles are produced each day and sold within minutes of being made. They are very cheap to buy, and some shops have a 'happy hour' during which all noodles are sold at half price.

Dried rice noodles, which are readily available in supermarkets and grocery stores, come in a variety of thicknesses. The finest rice vermicelli needs only to be soaked in hot tap water for about 10 minutes, or dropped into boiling water for 1 or 2 minutes. Flatter and thicker rice sticks need soaking in boiling water for 10 minutes.

Egg noodles (*ba mee*) are made from wheat flour and eggs. Introduced by the Chinese, they are readily available in Western countries. Often they are coiled in small bundles and it never does tell you on the packet that if you drop them directly into boiling water many of the strands stay firmly stuck together and will not cook properly. It's easy to prevent this happening. Immerse the bundles of noodles in a bowl of warm water from the tap and let them soak and loosen while a pot of water is put on to boil. Then drain the noodles, drop them into the boiling water and cook for 2 or 3 minutes, testing every 30 seconds, until tender but not mushy. Drain well in a colander.

Transparent noodles (*woon sen*) made from mung bean starch are very popular in Thailand. They are also called cellophane noodles. Because these noodles are extremely tough and difficult to cut when dry, dividing up a large bundle is sheer hard work. I suggest buying them in small bundles rather than large ones. But if you do have to cut off a small amount, sharp scissors work better than a knife. Soak in hot water or boil, as required in individual recipes.

Rice
(Khao)

2½ cups (1 lb) long grain rice

3½ cups (28 fl oz) water

There is no trick to cooking perfect, fluffy rice. It is all a matter of correct proportions, and if the same cup is used to measure rice and water, all will be well. For best results, use first grade, long grain 'jasmine' rice grown in Thailand. It has a faint natural perfume and the grains remain separate. No salt is added as the sauces served with it are salty enough.

I have outlined a couple of methods used in Thailand to cook rice. You will not find the rapid boil water-bath method here because no Asian cook would even consider it. Besides, the rice tastes so much better and retains more nutrition when cooked by any of the following methods.

Though I have given cup measurements for rice and water, it will be useful to know that there is just on 2½ standard measuring cups in a 500 g (1 lb) packet of rice (in case you don't choose to buy rice in bulk.) This quantity gives 4–6 main course servings when eating rice in the Thai manner, as the basis of the meal.

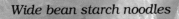

Wide bean starch noodles

Fine bean starch noodles

Rice paper sheets

Thin egg
noodles

White glutinous rice

Black glutinous rice

Thick egg noodles

Jasmine rice

Bean curd skins (background)

Rice noodles

Rice sticks

Rice noodles

Rice noodles

Steamer method

If the rice needs washing, wash well in cold water, drain in a colander and leave to dry for at least 30 minutes. Use a saucepan which is wide rather than deep and narrow, and which holds about 2 litres (8 cups). Put in the rice and the measured water, bring to the boil and cook over medium heat, uncovered, for about 6 minutes or until the water is absorbed. Holes will appear on the surface of the rice.

Have ready a steamer with boiling water (or a large pot into which a colander fits). Scoop the rice from the saucepan into the steamer or colander and steam over boiling water for 20 minutes. The rice grains will be perfectly cooked, firm and separate. Remove the steamer and serve the rice in a covered bowl or rice basket to keep warm.

Absorption method

Cooking by absorption in a pan with a well-fitting lid is both quicker and simpler than steaming, but it is essential that the heat can be turned very low, because the rice can stick to the pan and scorch.

2 tablespoons oil
4 spring onions (scallions), chopped
2 fresh chillies, seeded and sliced
1 tablespoon Red Curry Paste (*page 20*)
125 g (4 oz) uncooked medium-sized prawns (shrimp), shelled and deveined
1 cup fresh or frozen crab meat
2 cups cold steamed rice
1 tablespoon fish sauce
1 tablespoon lime or lemon juice
1 clove garlic, crushed

Omelettes:

8 eggs
½ teaspoon salt
2 tablespoons water
2 tablespoons oil
spring onion tops to garnish

Crab fried rice in omelette
(Kai Yud Sai Khao Poo)

Serves 4

Heat a wok, pour in the oil and on medium heat fry the spring onions and chillies, stirring, until softened. Add the red curry paste and cook, stirring, until fragrant. Add the prawns and stir-fry until they change colour. Stir in the crab meat and rice, tossing until heated through. Remove from heat. Combine the fish sauce, lime juice and garlic, and sprinkle over the rice, tossing to distribute seasoning. Put the rice in a bowl, cover and keep warm. Wash and dry the wok.

Beat the eggs with the salt and water. Heat the wok, add 2 teaspoons of oil and swirl to coat the surface. Pour in a quarter of the beaten egg mixture, lift the wok by the handles and swirl to make a large sheet of egg. Cook over low heat until almost set. Place a quarter of the rice mixture in the centre of the omelette and fold the edges over, envelope fashion, to enclose the rice. Press down well, slip a frying slice (wide metal spatula) underneath and gently turn it over. Drizzle a little oil down the side of the wok and lightly brown the other side. Lift onto a plate. Repeat with the remaining mixture. Dip the spring onion tops in boiling water until limp, and use to tie each omelette parcel.

Put the rice and water into a heavy-based pan, bring to the boil, then cover tightly and turn heat as low as it will go. Cook, without lifting the lid at all, for 15 minutes. The water should be completely absorbed. Remove from heat, uncover and let steam escape for a few minutes, then replace the lid to keep the rice warm.

If the rice is to be used for fried rice, turn it out onto a large tray as soon as cooking is completed, and leave to become completely cold and dry. Refrigerate overnight, uncovered, for best results.

Glutinous rice (KHAO NIEW)

In Northern Thailand, as in its neighbouring countries, sticky or glutinous rice is popular. For plain steamed sticky rice, soak the rice in cold water overnight and drain. Spread in a perforated steamer and steam over boiling water for 30 minutes, turning the rice over halfway through. If a richer result is desired, as soon as the rice has steamed, add it to 1 cup (8 fl oz) of hot coconut milk and leave, covered, for a further 30 minutes to absorb the milk. Reheat in the steamer.

125 g (4 oz) rice vermicelli
3 cups (24 fl oz) oil for deep-frying
½ cup finely minced (ground) pork or chicken
½ cup chopped prawns (shrimp)
1 cake yellow bean curd, finely diced
2 tablespoons white vinegar
2 tablespoons sugar
2 tablespoons fish sauce
2 eggs, beaten
2 tablespoons sliced pickled garlic
1 finely sliced red chilli
½ cup fresh coriander (cilantro/Chinese parsley)

Deep-fried crispy rice noodles
(Mee Grob)

This is *Mee Grob*, the dish by which a good Thai restaurant may be judged. The noodles should be snapping crisp, the flavours prominently sweet, hot, salty and sour, with more than a suspicion of garlic making impact. Many restaurants concentrate on the sweet flavour which is a pity.

Dip the rice vermicelli quickly in cold water, shake off the excess and leave it near a window to dry for at least 30 minutes. Separate it into small handfuls.

Heat the oil in a wok and when a light haze rises from the surface, test the heat with a few strands of the noodles. They should puff and swell to many times their size. If they don't, wait until the oil is hot enough or the noodles will be tough instead of crisp and light. Be ready to scoop them out as soon as they turn a pale gold and drain them well on several sheets of absorbent paper. Cool completely.

Pour off the oil into a heatproof bowl, leaving only about 2 tablespoons in the wok. Add the pork or chicken and fry, stirring constantly, until the colour changes. Add the prawns and cook for a further minute, then add the bean curd and toss until heated through. Add the vinegar, sugar and fish sauce, stirred together until the sugar has dissolved. When the mixture boils add the beaten eggs and keep on stirring until the egg is set and firm. This recipe may be prepared ahead to this stage, but heat it through before serving.

Just before serving, combine the crisp-fried noodles with the hot mixture. Scatter the pickled garlic, chilli and coriander leaves over to garnish, and serve immediately.

3 cups (24 fl oz) iced water

12–15 jasmine flowers

petals from 1 fragrant rose

4 cups cold cooked rice

crushed ice

Accompaniments:

Fried Prawn Balls (*page 96*)

Sweet and Hot Crisp Beef
(*page 136*)

Stuffed Capsicum in Egg Net
(*page 31*)

Iced rice
(Khao Chae)

This is an example of palace cooking which has become accessible to everyone. When it was devised by the ladies of King Chulalongkorn's court, ice was a luxury because it had to be brought in by ship from Singapore. In hot weather, rice was served in water scented with jasmine and rose petals, with crushed ice. Today, one can buy this dish at more plebian food stalls. But, as of old, the highly flavoured dishes which accompany the rice are intended to tempt jaded appetites.
Serves 4

Have the accompaniments prepared and ready. If possible, let the flowers steep in the water overnight, in a covered bowl in the refrigerator. Alternatively, add a few drops of jasmine or rose essence.

Put the completely cold rice in a serving bowl, pour the scented water over and add the crushed ice and a few blossoms. Serve, before the ice melts, with the accompaniments.

2 cups cooked and drained
bean starch vermicelli

½ teaspoon crushed garlic

2 tablespoons salted peanuts,
chopped

2 tablespoons fish sauce

1 tablespoon chopped spring
onions (scallions)

2 tablespoons chopped fresh
coriander (cilantro/Chinese
parsley)

juice of half a lime

2 red chillies, finely chopped
(optional)

2 teaspoons dried shrimp
powder

2 teaspoons Oriental peanut
oil (*see* Note)

Cold bean thread salad
(Yum Woon Sen)

Serves 2

Cut the vermicelli into short lengths and put into a bowl. Add all the other ingredients and mix together well.

Note:
Oriental peanut oil is unrefined peanut oil which has a distinctive flavour. Available at Asian stores. Please see Glossary.

Iced rice and accompaniments

1 cup uncooked rice
4 tablespoons cooked rice
1 cup grated fresh coconut
pinch of salt
1 tablespoon sugar
3 cups (24 fl oz) boiling water
oil

Topping:

½ cup (4 fl oz) thick coconut milk
2 tablespoons sugar
¼ teaspoon salt
2 tablespoons chopped spring onions (scallions)
2 tablespoons corn kernels
2 tablespoons pounded dried shrimp

Rice and coconut pancakes
(Khanom Krok)

These creamy rice cakes are baked in a pan that has round indentations similar to a gem iron (photographed opposite), used for gem scones in Australia; or an *aebelskiver* pan, which Danish cooks use and which is probably more common in Europe and the United States. They may be placed over a gas flame or electric hotplate.
Makes about 24

Put the first 5 ingredients into a bowl, pour the boiling water over and leave to get cold. Then blend at high speed in an electric blender until very finely ground. Mix the coconut milk, sugar and salt together.

Heat the gem iron or similar pan and brush with oil. Pour a small ladle of the rice mixture into each hollow, to almost fill. Cook over low heat or in a hot oven, 220°C (425°F/Gas 7), until firm. Top each with a teaspoon of the coconut milk mixture. Add a sprinkling of chopped spring onions, a few corn kernels, or some dried shrimp powder and finish by cooking a further minute or two. Run a small spatula between the pan and each cake to loosen, and if the outside is well browned and crisp, remove to a wire rack. Serve warm.

125 g (4 oz) rice sticks
250 g (8 oz) chicken thigh fillets
3 tablespoons peanut oil
1 teaspoon crushed garlic
½ cup very tiny dried shrimp
2 teaspoons chilli radish, chopped
1 teaspoon black bean sauce with chilli (*see* Note, *page 159*)
2 tablespoons fish sauce
1 tablespoon chilli sauce
1 tablespoon lime juice

Garnish:

½ cup chopped fresh coriander (cilantro/Chinese parsley)
½ cup roasted, salted peanuts, chopped

Rice noodles with chicken and prawns
(Kway Teo Phat Gai Goong)

Serves 4

Pour boiling water over the rice sticks, cover and allow to soak for 10 minutes. Drain in a colander. Remove the skin and any visible fat from the chicken, and cut the flesh into thin slices.

Heat a wok or frying pan, add the oil and fry the garlic until golden, stirring constantly. Add the dried prawns and fry, stirring, for 1 minute. Add the chilli radish and black bean sauce, stir well and turn in the chicken. Stir-fry until the chicken has changed colour. Pour in the fish sauce, chilli sauce and lime juice mixed together and toss in the rice noodles, mixing well. Mix half of the coriander and peanuts through. Serve hot and sprinkle the remaining garnishes over.

Rice and coconut pancakes

1 cup (6 oz) short grain rice
1½ cups (12 fl oz) water
oil for deep-frying

Deep-fried rice crackers with dips
(Khao Tang-Na Tang)

If the rice sticks at the bottom of the pot, Thai cooks turn it into a delicious snack. It is so popular that now it is a dish in its own right.
Serves 8

Put the rice and water in a saucepan and boil, uncovered, until holes appear in the rice mass. Turn heat very low, cover the pan tightly and cook for 15 minutes. Cool.

Grease a large tray, spread rice out on the tray and flatten to a thin layer, with a hand dipped in water. Mark into triangles or squares with a wet knife and bake in a very slow oven, 130°C (275°F/Gas 2) until completely dry, about 1 hour.

Remove from the oven and cool, then break into the marked pieces. Store in an airtight container. Just before serving, deep-fry in hot oil until golden. Drain on absorbent paper. Serve with Shrimp Dip with Tamarind (*page 84*) and/or Pork and Peanut Dip (*page 84*).

1 x 100 g (3½ oz) pkt bean starch vermicelli
185 g (6 oz) chicken thigh fillets
1 egg
½ teaspoon crushed garlic
2 teaspoons hot pickled bamboo shoot
1 onion, finely sliced
2 tablespoons dried shrimp (either tiny ones in shells, or larger dried shrimp, pounded)
¼ cup roughly chopped spring onions (scallions), or garlic chives
3 tablespoons peanut oil

Seasoning:

1 tablespoon sweet chilli sauce
2 tablespoons fish sauce
1 teaspoon sugar
2 tablespoons lime juice

Garnish:

¼ cup fresh coriander
½ cup crushed roasted peanuts
1 red chilli, finely sliced, or 1 teaspoon crushed dried chilli

Bean starch noodles with chicken
(Kai Phad Woon Sen)

Thai food is so full of flavour, it is possible to make a light meal for two or three people using the quantity of meat or poultry that would feed one person in a Western-style dish.
Serves 2–3

Drop the noodles into boiling water and cook for 10 minutes. Drain in a colander and cut into short lengths. Remove all skin and fat from the chicken and cut the meat into fine slices. Beat the egg and have all these ready to hand.

Put the measured garlic, bamboo shoot and onion on a plate in separate mounds. Have the dried shrimp and spring onions measured in small bowls. Combine the seasoning ingredients in a bowl and stir to dissolve the sugar.

Heat a wok and add the oil. Add the garlic and stir-fry for a few seconds, then add the bamboo shoot and onion and continue to fry for a minute longer. Add the dried shrimp and spring onions, fry for 30 seconds and then add the chicken, turning it constantly until all the pinkness has disappeared and it is cooked. With this small amount of chicken, it should take only 2 minutes on high heat.

Add the mixed seasonings and stir well, turn in the noodles and keep tossing until evenly mixed. Add half the garnish ingredients and stir through. Serve sprinkled with the remaining garnishes.

Deep fried rice crackers.
Shrimp dip with tamarind.
Pork and peanut dip

1.5 litres (6 cups) pork or chicken soup Stock (*page 50*)
125 g (4 oz) minced (ground) pork
125 g (4 oz) chicken or pork, finely sliced
2 tablespoons dried shrimp
2 or 3 cubes fried bean curd, sliced
125 g (4 oz) rice noodles, soaked and drained
2 teaspoons palm sugar
2 tablespoons fish sauce
2 tablespoons lime juice
1 cup bean sprouts

Accompaniments:

2 tablespoons preserved radish, shredded
¼ cup crushed peanuts
½ cup chopped fresh coriander (cilantro/Chinese parsley)
1 tablespoon fried garlic flakes
2 tablespoons fried shallots
sliced hot chillies in fish sauce
crushed dried chillies (optional)

Floating market soup noodles
(Kway Teo Ruer)

Of course you can buy and eat these noodles elsewhere, but they'll always remind me of breakfast at the floating market at Damnernsaduak. Sitting on wooden steps leading down to the canal and eating the noodles with chopsticks, we enjoyed watching the lady vendor deftly cook each serving separately. Wearing the typical wide-brimmed bamboo hat, she gracefully balanced herself in her boat as it swayed and dipped in the wash of other boats going past and was delighted when we asked for the accompaniments of hot chillies and salty *nam pla* just like the local customers.
Serves 4

Bring 1 cup (8 fl oz) of the stock to the boil, add the minced pork and stir while cooking to break up any lumps. Add the sliced chicken or pork and the remaining stock, and simmer until tender. Add the dried shrimp, the bean curd and rice noodles. Stir in the palm sugar, fish sauce, lime juice and bean sprouts. Simmer for 2 minutes. Taste and add more fish sauce or lime juice if necessary.

Serve the noodles and soup in bowls, topped with a little of each of the accompaniments, and let each person help themselves to the chillies.

Note:
Fried shallots (sometimes labelled 'red onions') may be bought in tubs or packets, ready to use. Store in the freezer. They will not need heating. Dried garlic flakes need to be fried for just a few seconds in medium-hot oil.

Floating market soup noodles

Fried noodles with barbecued pork

4 dried *shiitake* mushrooms
2 tablespoons soy sauce
2 teaspoons sugar
150 g (5 oz) barbecued pork
1 tablespoon salted black beans
5 bundles thin egg noodles
3 tablespoons peanut oil
1 teaspoon finely chopped garlic
1 teaspoon finely grated fresh ginger
3 fresh chillies, sliced
3 spring onions (scallions), sliced, with green tops
2 tablespoons fish sauce
2 tablespoons lime juice

Accompaniments:

crisp-fried onions
crushed roasted peanuts
crushed dried chillies
sliced fresh chillies
2 tablespoons fish sauce
2 tablespoons lime juice
1 teaspoon sugar

Fried egg noodles with barbecued pork
(Ba Mee Phat Moo Yang)

The Chinese influence shows in this dish, tempered by the ever-present Thai flavourings of chilli, fish sauce and lime juice.
Serves 4–6

Soak the dried mushrooms in 1 cup (8 fl oz) hot water for 30 minutes, then drain, reserving the water. Discard the stems. Slice the caps and simmer 15 minutes in the soaking water with the soy sauce and sugar.

Cut the barbecued pork into thin slices. Rinse the salted black beans in a small strainer under the cold tap for a few seconds to remove excess salt.

Put water on to boil for cooking the noodles. Place the noodles in a bowl, run hot water from the tap to cover them and leave to soak for 10 minutes or until the strands separate. Drain, and drop into the boiling water. Cook for 2 or 3 minutes, just until tender. Drain well.

Heat the oil in a wok and fry the garlic and ginger for a few seconds without browning. Add the black beans and chillies and fry for a few minutes. Toss in the noodles, barbecued pork, mushrooms and spring onions, sprinkle with the fish sauce and lime juice and toss until evenly mixed. Serve with the accompaniments in small bowls – the first three are kept separate, and the sliced fresh chillies are mixed with the fish sauce, lime juice and sugar.

Note:
Crisp-fried onions may be bought from Asian food stores. Store in the freezer.

250 g (8 oz) rice vermicelli
185 g (6 oz) chicken or beef
3 tablespoons peanut oil
1 teaspoon chopped garlic
2 teaspoons fermented soy beans with sesame
½ teaspoon black bean sauce with chilli (*see* Note)

Seasonings:

1 tablespoon sweet chilli sauce
2 tablespoons fish sauce
1 tablespoon lime juice

Garnish:

¼ cup chopped fresh coriander
1 tablespoon fried garlic flakes (*page 209*)
1 teaspoon dried chilli flakes

Rice noodles with hot seasonings
(Sen Mee Phat Nuer)

Serves 4

Put the rice vermicelli in a bowl and run very hot water from the tap to cover. Soak for 10 minutes, then drain. Cut the chicken or beef into fine shreds. Measure the other ingredients and have everything ready to hand. Mix the seasonings together.

Heat a wok and add the oil, fry the garlic until golden, stirring constantly. Add the fermented beans and the black bean sauce and stir quickly, then add the chicken or beef and cook until the colour changes. Pour in the seasoning mixture, stir and allow to come to the boil. Turn in the drained vermicelli and mix thoroughly with half the garnish ingredients. Serve and sprinkle the remaining garnishes on top.

Note:
'Black bean sauce with chilli' is my description of an ingredient which is known – apart from the Oriental characters – by the French name *sauce de soja au piment*. It is very hot, and should be approached with caution!

The fermented soy beans with sesame are also sold in jars in Asian stores.

250 g (8 oz) fine rice vermicelli
6 dried *shiitake* mushrooms
2 tablespoons wood fungus
125 g (4 oz) fried bean curd squares or fermented soy beans (*tempeh*)
125 g (4 oz) fresh bean sprouts
1 cup fine julienne strips of carrot
a few tender asparagus tips, blanched
2 cups finely shredded cabbage
3 tablespoons peanut oil
1 teaspoon crushed garlic
1 teaspoon finely grated fresh ginger
2 tablespoons Golden Mountain Sauce (*see* Glossary, *page 210*), or light soy sauce
2 teaspoons sugar
radish flower
chilli sauce

Whole Earth vegetarian noodles
(Phat Mee Jeh)

This recipe is reconstructed from memory after a delicious vegetarian meal at the Whole Earth restaurant in Chiang Mai, and has been taste-tested at home.
Serves 4

Put the noodles into a bowl and pour boiling water over. Leave to soak for 2 or 3 minutes, then drain. Test by biting a piece. The very fine variety will be done in the shorter time.

Soak the dried mushrooms in very hot water for 30 minutes, squeeze out excess water, discard the stems and cut caps into thin strips. Soak the wood fungus in cold water for 10 minutes, cut off any gritty portions, and divide into bite-sized pieces.

Dice or slice the bean curd or, if using *tempeh*, cut in thin slices and then into fine strips. Wash and drain the bean sprouts and pinch off any straggly tails. Set all these ingredients, together with the carrot strips, asparagus tips and shredded cabbage, on a plate in separate piles, reserving some bean sprouts and shredded cabbage for garnish.

Heat a wok, add the oil and swirl to coat the wok. On medium heat fry the garlic and ginger, stirring, until golden (about 1 minute). Add the bean curd or *tempeh* and fry. Add the mushrooms and ½ cup (4 fl oz) water, then stir in the sauce and sugar and simmer for 10 minutes. There should be about ¼ cup (2 fl oz) liquid. If necessary add a little more water.

Add the wood fungus, bean sprouts, carrots, asparagus tips and shredded cabbage and toss for a minute, then turn in the noodles and mix well. Cover and steam for 3 or 4 minutes to heat through. Toss vigorously again to mix all the ingredients and serve hot, garnished with the reserved bean sprouts and shredded cabbage, and a radish flower. Chilli sauce is served separately as a flavour accent.

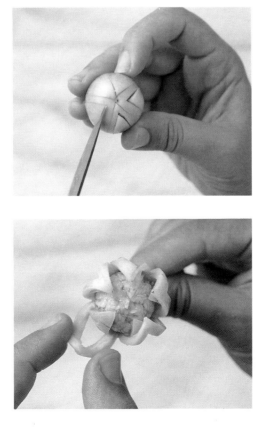

Whole earth vegetarian noodles

3 eggs, beaten

salt and pepper

3 tablespoons peanut oil

1 onion, finely chopped

1 teaspoon crushed garlic

2 fresh hot chillies, sliced

1 pork chop, finely diced, or
   1 diced chicken breast

250 g (8 oz) raw prawns
   (shrimp)

4 cups cold cooked rice

125 g (4 oz) frozen crab meat,
   or meat from 1 cooked
   crab

2 tablespoons fish sauce, or to
   taste

2 tablespoons chilli sauce, or
   to taste

chilli flower

---

2 dried *shiitake* mushrooms

250 g (8 oz) pork mince

1 teaspoon Pepper and
   Coriander Paste (*page 23*)

2 tablespoons finely chopped
   canned bamboo shoot

2 tablespoons finely chopped
   canned water chestnuts

1 tablespoon plain (all-
   purpose) flour

2 bundles egg noodles, about
   100 g (3½ oz)

Curry:

1½ cups (12 fl oz) coconut
   milk

1 tablespoon Green Curry
   Paste (*page 21*)

2 teaspoons finely chopped
   garlic

2 teaspoons fish sauce

1 tablespoon seeded and
   sliced chillies

1 teaspoon palm sugar

3 tablespoons sliced spring
   onions (scallions)

fresh coriander

chilli flowers

Mixed fried rice
(Khao Phat Ruam Mit)

Making fried rice is like jazz improvising – anything goes. Well, almost anything. This recipe is intended as a guide, but feel free to substitute ingredients as available.
Serves 4

Season the beaten eggs with salt and pepper to taste. Heat a wok or frying pan and grease lightly with 1 teaspoon of the peanut oil. Pour in some of the beaten egg, swirl to coat the pan and cook on low heat until set but not browned. Remove to a plate and repeat with the remaining beaten egg. Set aside to cool, then roll up and cut into fine strips.

Heat the remaining oil in the wok and fry the onion and garlic, stirring frequently, until golden. Add half the sliced chillies and toss for a few seconds, then fry the diced pork or chicken until well cooked. Add the prawns and stir-fry until the colour changes. Add the rice and toss over high heat until heated through. Add the crab meat, fish sauce and chilli sauce and toss constantly for a further minute or two. Serve sprinkled with the remaining sliced chillies and garnished with the omelette strips and a chilli flower.

Pork balls with noodles
(Ba Mee Look Chin Moo)

Serves 4

Soak the mushrooms in hot water for at least 30 minutes. Drain and chop finely. Put into a bowl with the next 5 ingredients and mix well. Shape the mixture into small balls about 4 cm (1½ in) in diameter and set aside. Cook the noodles in fast boiling water until tender, drain and rinse in cold water.

In a wok heat half the coconut milk, stir in the green curry paste and garlic, and cook until fragrant. Stir in the remaining coconut milk and when boiling drop in the pork balls a few at a time.

Reduce heat and simmer the pork balls 8–10 minutes. Gently stir in the fish sauce, chillies and palm sugar. Drain the noodles and gently stir into the curry. Cook 2–3 minutes. Serve hot, garnished with spring onions, fresh coriander leaves and chilli flowers. It may be necessary to add more coconut milk or hot water if the curry is too thick.

Mixed fried rice

Vegetables

Visiting the markets in Thailand was a real eye-opener.
There were mushrooms I had never seen before and others
which hitherto I had found only in cans; fresh bamboo
shoots still wearing their fuzzy wrappings; tender green
asparagus in huge bunches; green pawpaws; gourds of
many shapes and sizes; pendulous purple banana flowers
which are used as a vegetable; winged beans, snake beans,
okra beans, sataw beans; chillies of all shapes, sizes and
colours; and everywhere, the small bunches of herbs and
flavourings I can only describe as a Thai 'bouquet garni'
. . . stems of lemon grass, slices of fresh turmeric and
galangal, and several kaffir lime leaves.

To the vegetable vendors, it seemed not at all
incongruous that mundane vegetables sat side by side with
huge piles of exotic, dew-fresh orchids that — in any
florist's shop in the West would carry a price high enough
to purchase their entire stock !

250 g (8 oz) firm green cabbage

125 g (4 oz) pork loin or rib chop

125 g (4 oz) raw prawns (shrimp)

1 tablespoon oil

1 teaspoon Pepper and Coriander Paste (*page 23*)

1 or 2 red chillies, sliced

1 teaspoon sugar

1 tablespoon fish sauce

1 teaspoon cornflour (cornstarch)

Cabbage with prawns and pork loin
(Moo Goong, Kalum Plee)
Serves 4–6

Trim the cabbage and cut into approximately 2.5 cm x 5 cm (1 in x 2 in) blocks. Cut the pork loin into small dice. Shell and devein the prawns.

Heat the oil and cook the pepper and coriander paste for a minute or two. Add the pork and fry until crisp, then the prawns and stir-fry for 1 minute. Stir in the cabbage and chillies, cover and cook for 3 or 4 minutes. Add the sugar and fish sauce. Thicken the liquid with cornflour blended with a tablespoon of cold water. Serve with rice.

---

6 slender young eggplants (aubergines)

125 g (4 oz) raw prawn (shrimp) meat

125 g (4 oz) chicken breast fillets

½ cup finely chopped spring onions (scallions)

2 teaspoons garlic, finely chopped

1 red or green chilli, finely chopped

1 tablespoon finely chopped coriander (cilantro/Chinese parsley) leaves

1 stem lemon grass, finely chopped

2 tablespoons fish sauce

chilli sauce

Batter:

1 egg

3 tablespoons water

3 tablespoons rice flour

3 tablespoons plain (all-purpose) flour

oil for deep-frying

Filled and fried eggplant
(Makua Sod Sai Tod)

Slender eggplants, which are no wider than a gherkin, though a little longer, and which are becoming more readily available here, are the right kind to use for this recipe, not the large ones.
Serves 6

Halve the eggplants lengthways and sprinkle with salt. Leave for 20 minutes to degorge, then pat dry on paper towels. Scoop out each centre, leaving a thin shell. Chop the centres finely and mix with the remaining ingredients, except for the chilli sauce. Fill the eggplants with the mixture, packing firmly.

Prepare a batter by combining the egg, water and both kinds of flour. Heat the oil in a wok or frying pan. Coat each eggplant with the batter and slide into the oil, then fry on medium-high heat until golden brown. Drain on absorbent paper and serve with chilli sauce.

Cabbage with prawns and pork loin

6 slices galangal, fresh, frozen or dried

3 kaffir lime leaves

10 squares of fried bean curd

2½ cups (20 fl oz) thin coconut milk

1 teaspoon Pepper and Coriander Paste (*page 23*)

2 stems lemon grass, thinly sliced

3 fresh green chillies

1 teaspoon salt

1 tablespoon fish sauce, or light soy sauce

lime juice to taste

1 cup (8 fl oz) thick coconut milk

1 teaspoon sugar

¼ cup finely chopped fresh coriander (cilantro/Chinese parsley)

2 red chillies, sliced

Fried bean curd in coconut milk
(Tao Hu Tom Kha)

This is a vegetarian version of the popular chicken dish, *Tom Kha gai*, which features a galangal-flavoured coconut sauce.
Serves 4–6

If using dried galangal (*kha*) and kaffir lime leaves, soak them in hot water for 30 minutes. Cut the squares of bean curd in halves diagonally, then cut each piece in half again to give thin triangular slices.

Put the galangal, thin coconut milk, pepper and coriander paste, lemon grass, green chillies, salt, lime leaves and fish sauce into a saucepan and bring gently to the boil, stirring. Simmer for 10 minutes, then add the bean curd and simmer for a further 10 minutes.

Stir in the lime juice, thick coconut milk and sugar, and continue simmering for a few minutes longer, until the sauce is thick and reduced. Sprinkle with the coriander and red chillies, and serve with rice.

Fried bean curd in coconut milk and stir-fried water chestnuts and snow peas

Stir-fried water chestnuts and snow peas
(Pad Haeo Chine, Tua Lun Tao)

Serves 4–6

125 g (4 oz) snow peas (*mange-tout*)
1 x 185 g (6 oz) can sliced water chestnuts
2 tablespoons oil
1 teaspoon finely chopped garlic
1 tablespoon fish sauce
1 tablespoon Golden Mountain Sauce (*see* Glossary, *page 210*)
1 teaspoon sugar
½ cup (4 fl oz) stock, or water
2 teaspoons cornflour (cornstarch)

String the snow peas and drain the liquid from the water chestnuts. If unable to purchase them already sliced, cut the water chestnuts into two or three discs.

Heat the oil in a wok or frying pan and on a low heat fry the garlic, stirring, until it is just starting to change colour. Add the snow peas and toss for 1 minute, then add the water chestnuts, and the sauces, sugar and stock stirred together.

When it comes to the boil, stir in the cornflour mixed smoothly with a tablespoon of cold water. Stir constantly until it boils and thickens. Serve with rice.

Water convolvulus with dried shrimp
(Pak Boong Phad Goong Haeng)

250 g (8 oz) water convolvulus (*kang kung*)
½ cup dried shrimp
1 tablespoon oil
1 teaspoon finely chopped garlic
1 teaspoon finely chopped fresh ginger
1 tablespoon oyster sauce

Wash the vegetable well, shake off any surplus water and cut into 5 cm (2 in) lengths. Soak the dried shrimp in hot water to cover for about 10 minutes, drain, and pound lightly in a mortar and pestle.

Heat the oil and cook the garlic and ginger until golden. Stir in the shrimp and water convolvulus, and stir-fry for only a couple of minutes. Stir in the oyster sauce and serve immediately with rice.

Fried bean curd and mixed vegetables
(Tao Hu Phad Pak Pason)

Serves 4

½ cup peeled pumpkin, cut into 4 cm (1½ in) strips
½ cup celery, sliced
½ cup fresh asparagus, cut into 4 cm (1½ in) lengths
1 x 425 g (13½ oz) can young corn cobs, drained
½ cup snow peas (*mange-tout*), strings removed
4 pieces black fungus, soaked for 10 minutes
1 tablespoon oil
1 teaspoon finely chopped garlic
3–4 squares fried bean curd, each cut into 8 pieces
1 tablespoon fish sauce or light soy sauce
1 medium chilli, finely sliced

Prepare all the vegetables and have them ready in separate bowls. Trim any gritty pieces from the drained black fungus, then cut the fungus into pieces.

Heat the oil in a wok and fry the garlic until golden. Add the pumpkin and celery, and toss over heat for 4 or 5 minutes. Toss in the asparagus, young corn cobs, snow peas, black fungus and bean curd, and stir-fry for a further 5 minutes. Cover and cook on medium heat until the vegetables are tender but still crisp. Season with the fish sauce and garnish with sliced chilli. Serve with rice or noodles.

250 g (8 oz) slender eggplants (aubergines)
125 g (4 oz) *tempeh*
3 tablespoons oil
1 teaspoon finely chopped garlic
2 teaspoons Pepper and Coriander Paste (*page 23*)
1–2 tablespoons fish sauce, or light soy sauce
1 teaspoon palm sugar
2 teaspoons lime juice
1 or 2 red chillies, finely sliced, or 2 whole red chillies, fried

Stir-fried eggplant with *tempeh*
(Makua Phad Tempeh)
Serves 4

Wash the eggplants and with a stainless steel knife cut them into 2 cm (¾ in) dice. Thaw the *tempeh* and steam for 10 minutes, then cut in thin slices.

Heat the oil and fry the garlic, and pepper and coriander paste, stirring constantly, until fragrant. Add the *tempeh* and fry until golden brown, then remove it and set aside. Add the eggplants and fry until golden, adding more oil if necessary. Stir in the fish sauce, palm sugar and lime juice, then return the fried *tempeh*. Mix together well and serve sprinkled with sliced chillies, or place a couple of fried whole chillies on top.

500 g (1 lb) asparagus
2 cloves finely chopped garlic
1 teaspoon green peppercorns, crushed
1 tablespoon fish sauce
1–2 tablespoons Golden Mountain Sauce (*see Glossary, page 210*) or oyster sauce
2 teaspoons sugar
2 tablespoons oil
2 red chillies, finely sliced

Stir-fried asparagus
(Phad Nor Mai Farang)

I always thought of asparagus as being a very European vegetable, and was surprised to see some of the freshest, greenest, highest quality asparagus in the markets in Thailand.
Serves 4

Trim the asparagus and peel the lower stalks. Cut into bite-sized pieces. Combine the garlic, peppercorns, sauces and sugar, stirring to dissolve the sugar.

Heat the oil in a wok or frying pan, and on high heat stir-fry the asparagus until crisp and tender. Add the garlic mixture and chillies, mix well and serve at once.

500 g (1 lb) spinach
2 tablespoons oil
1 teaspoon finely chopped garlic
½ cup sliced spring onions (scallions)
¼ teaspoon freshly ground black pepper
2 tablespoons Golden Mountain Sauce (*see Glossary, page 210*)
1 red chilli, finely sliced

Stir-fried spinach
(Phad Pak Kom)
Serves 4

Wash the spinach well and remove the tough stems. Heat the oil and cook the garlic and spring onions until golden. Gently stir-fry the spinach until just wilted. Sprinkle with the pepper and Golden Mountain sauce.

Garnish with sliced chilli and serve immediately as spinach is very sensitive to heat, and will darken unattractively if left to stand.

Stir-fried eggplant with tempeh and stir-fried asparagus

Bean curd in cabbage rolls
(Kalum Plee Pan Tao Hu)

Makes 6 rolls

400 g (13 oz) soft bean curd

6 green cabbage leaves

6 spring onion (scallion) tops

1 tablespoon oil

250 g (8 oz) minced (ground) beef

2 tablespoons fish sauce

2 tablespoons palm sugar

1 teaspoon Pepper and Coriander Paste (*page 23*)

¼ cup chopped garlic chives, or spring onions (scallions)

1 egg, beaten

1 cup (8 fl oz) stock

2 tablespoons Golden Mountain Sauce (*see Glossary, page 210*)

2 teaspoons rice flour

2 tablespoons lime juice

Garnish:

sliced chillies

fresh coriander (cilantro/Chinese parsley)

Drain all the water from the bean curd and lift out the squares onto a double thickness of kitchen paper. Leave to drain thoroughly.

With a sharp knife remove the hard centre leaf ribs and cut the cabbage leaves in halves if they are large. Plunge the leaves into boiling water to soften, then cool quickly in cold water. Drain well. Plunge the spring onion tops into boiling water to soften, cool in cold water and set aside.

Heat the oil and fry the beef until the colour changes. Add a tablespoon each of the fish sauce and palm sugar. Add the pepper and coriander paste and continue cooking until the meat is tender. Mix in the bean curd and garlic chives. Reduce the heat and stir in the egg. Divide the mixture between the cabbage leaves and roll up each one like a parcel, tucking in the ends. Secure each roll by tying with the softened spring onion tops. Place the rolls in a pan and pour around them the stock mixed with the Golden Mountain sauce and the remaining palm sugar.

Simmer for 20–25 minutes, or until the cabbage is tender. Drain the rolls and place on a serving plate. Blend the rice flour with the remaining tablespoon of fish sauce, mix into the stock and stir until thick. Stir in the lime juice, then pour over the rolls. Garnish with the sliced chillies and the coriander.

Eggplant with bean curd
(Phad Ma Kua Tao Hu)

Serves 4–6

250 g (8 oz) slender eggplants (aubergines)

3 tablespoons oil

2 teaspoons finely chopped garlic

250 g (8 oz) soft bean curd, drained

1 teaspoon palm sugar

1 tablespoon lime juice

1 tablespoon fish sauce

4 red chillies, seeded and sliced

½ cup basil leaves

Wash the eggplants, but do not peel them. Slice the eggplants into thin diagonal slices. Heat the oil, add the eggplants and garlic, and stir-fry until golden. Stir in the bean curd and cook a further 2 minutes, or until golden.

Gently stir in the combined palm sugar, lime juice and fish sauce, chillies and basil leaves. Serve as part of a meal with rice and other dishes.

4 medium-sized banana capsicums (sweet peppers)
125 g (4 oz) minced (ground) pork
60 g (2 oz) raw prawns (shrimp), chopped
1 teaspoon garlic, finely chopped
1 teaspoon Pepper and Coriander Paste (*page 23*)
1¼ cups (10 fl oz) coconut milk
2 tablespoons Red Curry Paste (*page 20*)
2 teaspoons palm sugar
1 tablespoon fish sauce
1 teaspoon paprika
2 or 3 lime leaves
½ cup basil leaves
2 red chillies, sliced

Banana capsicum curry
(Kaeng Prik Yuak Sod Sai)

Banana capsicums are an ideal size for filling with savoury mixtures, and their flavour is distinctive without being pungent.
Serves 4

Cut the tops off the capsicums and remove the seeds and pith. Combine the pork, prawns, garlic, and pepper and coriander paste, and pack into the capsicums with a teaspoon.

Heat half the coconut milk and cook the red curry paste until fragrant. Stir in the remaining coconut milk, sugar, fish sauce, paprika and lime leaves.

Place the capsicums in the simmering sauce and cook for 20–25 minutes, or until tender, turning after 10–15 minutes. Place them on a plate and stir the basil leaves and chillies into the sauce before pouring it over the capsicums.

125 g (4 oz) *tempeh*
½ cup (4 fl oz) peanut oil
2 cups (16 fl oz) coconut milk
1 tablespoon Red Curry Paste (*page 20*)
½ teaspoon grated kaffir lime rind
6 spring onions (scallions), cut into short lengths
1 teaspoon palm sugar
1 tablespoon fish sauce
20 fresh basil leaves
¼ cup fresh coriander (cilantro/Chinese parsley)
2 red or green chillies, sliced

Tempeh curry
(Lon Tempeh)

Tempeh is a high-protein ingredient in vegetarian diets, made from fermented soy beans pressed into a cake. Look for it in the freezer section of Asian or health food stores, usually in 250 g (8 oz) packets.
Serves 4

Thaw the *tempeh* if frozen, and cut into thin slices. Heat the oil in a wok or frying pan and fry the *tempeh* until crisp and golden. Drain on absorbent paper.

Pour off the oil, wipe out the wok and heat half the coconut milk until boiling. Add the curry paste with the lime rind, and cook until fragrant. Add the spring onions to the simmering mixture together with the fried *tempeh*. Stir in the remaining coconut milk and simmer, uncovered, for about 7 minutes. Stir in the palm sugar, fish sauce and basil leaves.

Serve hot over noodles or with rice, garnished with the coriander leaves and chillies.

2 medium eggplants
½ cup (2 oz) rice flour
½ teaspoon baking powder
½ teaspoon salt
1 egg yolk
½ cup (4 fl oz) coconut milk
oil for deep-frying

Eggplant in batter
(Makua Chup Pang Tod)

Wash but do not peel the eggplants, then slice thinly.

In a bowl combine the rest of the ingredients except the oil, and whisk to a smooth batter. Dip the sliced vegetable in the batter and deep-fry until crisp. Drain and serve immediately with *nam prik* sauce (*page 80*).

125 g (4 oz) cauliflower
125 g (4 oz) Thai spinach
4 spring onions (scallions)
2 coriander (cilantro/Chinese parsley) roots
1 teaspoon chopped garlic
½ teaspoon turmeric
1 tablespoon oil
1 yellow or red chilli, sliced

Cauliflower with Thai spinach
(Pad Pak Kom, Dok Galum)

Thai spinach (the same variety is used throughout Asia) is worth trying. I have placed some of the raw spinach around the photograph to make identification easy. If not available, use English spinach.
Serves 4

Wash the cauliflower and divide into florets. Wash the spinach, cut into 8 cm (3 in) lengths and blanch for a few seconds in boiling water, then refresh in cold water. Trim the spring onions and cut into 4 cm (1½ in) lengths, including part of the green tops.

Chop the coriander roots and pound to a paste in a mortar and pestle, together with the garlic and turmeric. Heat half the oil and fry the spring onions for a minute. Add the spinach and toss for a further minute, remove and set aside.

Heat the remaining oil and cook the coriander paste, stirring, until fragrant. Add the cauliflower and stir-fry for 4 or 5 minutes. Arrange on a dish, place the spinach and spring onions around, and serve garnished with sliced chilli.

2 or 3 medium-large zucchini (courgettes)

Filling:

250 g (8 oz) minced (ground) pork
125 g (4 oz) raw prawns (shrimp), shelled, deveined and chopped
¼ teaspoon finely grated lime rind
1 tablespoon fish sauce
1 teaspoon palm sugar
½ cup finely chopped spring onions (scallions)
2 teaspoons Pepper and Coriander Paste (*page 23*)

Coconut sauce:

¾ cup (6 fl oz) coconut milk
½ teaspoon salt
2 teaspoons rice flour

Garnish:

shredded kaffir lime leaf
chilli slices

Stuffed zucchini
(Sod Sai Zucchini)

Choose zucchini which are about 6–7 cm (2½–3 in) in diameter so there is room for an adequate amount of filling.
Serves 4–6

Wash the zucchini, top and tail them, then cut into 4 cm (1½ in) slices. Scoop out the centre of each slice, leaving a thin layer on the bottom.

Combine all the filling ingredients and fill each slice with 2 or 3 teaspoons of mixture. Steam for 15–20 minutes, or until tender but still holding their shape. Arrange on a serving plate. Spoon the coconut sauce over the slices and garnish with fine shreds of lime leaf and chilli slices.

Coconut sauce:
Combine the coconut milk, salt and rice flour in a small saucepan and cook, stirring, until it comes to the boil and thickens.

Cauliflower with Thai spinach and stuffed zucchini

1 ridged gourd, about 150 g (5 oz)
1 cup (8 fl oz) thick coconut milk
2 teaspoons Green Curry Paste (*page 21*)
1 tablespoon finely sliced lemon grass
1 tablespoon fish sauce
½ cup (4 fl oz) water
2 teaspoons lime juice
1 teaspoon palm sugar
1 or 2 fresh green chillies

Ridged gourd curry
(Gaeng Khiew Wan Buab Liam)

If you see this vegetable at the markets or in Asian stores, be prepared to give it a try — it is mild and sweet-flavoured, blending well with coconut milk and fresh herb flavours.
Serves 4–5

Wash the gourd well and use a vegetable peeler to remove the sharp edges from the ridges that run down the length of the vegetable. Cut into 4 cm (1½ in) slices.

Heat ½ cup (4 fl oz) coconut milk, add the curry paste and cook, stirring, until it smells fragrant. Add the lemon grass, fish sauce and water. Stir until it comes to the boil, then simmer for 2 or 3 minutes.

Add the slices of gourd, the lime juice, palm sugar and green chillies, and simmer until the gourd is tender. Stir in the remaining ½ cup coconut milk, heat through and serve with rice or noodles.

300 g (10 oz) mixed vegetables
2 cloves garlic
2 or 3 red chillies
1 stem lemon grass, finely sliced, or 2 strips lemon rind
2 kaffir lime leaves, or ½ teaspoon grated kaffir lime rind
1 cup (8 fl oz) coconut milk
1 tablespoon fish sauce
1 tablespoon lime juice
10 fresh basil leaves

Mixed vegetables in coconut milk
(Tom Kati Pak Ruam)

For this recipe, any fresh vegetables in season may be combined; cut them into pieces of similar size. Fresh asparagus is very popular in Thailand, so use it when available. Pumpkin, zucchini (courgettes), young corn cobs, celery, beans, water chestnuts, bamboo shoot and dried mushrooms which have been soaked and sliced are just some suggestions.
Serves 4–6

Prepare the vegetables by washing, peeling where necessary and cutting into pieces. Pound the garlic, chillies, lemon grass and lime rind to a paste. (If using lime leaves, simmer them whole with the vegetables and coconut milk.)

Heat half the coconut milk until oily and fry the paste until fragrant. Add the prepared vegetables and remaining coconut milk, with a little water if necessary. Simmer for 5 minutes, or until the vegetables are tender but crisp. Stir in the fish sauce, lime juice and basil leaves and serve with rice or noodles.

Ridged gourd curry and mixed vegetables in coconut milk

Thai Desserts
and Sweet Snacks

As in most Asian cuisines, desserts are not a feature of Thai meals but there is no denying that most people like to finish a meal with something sweet, whether it is fresh fruit or fruit juice or one of the fancier recipes featured here.

For the most part, these sweets are eaten as between-meal snacks. They are based mainly on rice flour or tapioca flour, coconut milk and palm sugar, mung beans and vegetables such as pumpkin and potato, and strongly flavoured fruits like mango and durian.

These are dainty mouthfuls and quite irresistible. Some of them are so simple that they can be made in almost no time compared to Western desserts. Others are fun to make if you have a little time to spare — for example, moulding the miniature fruits. Making them is as enjoyable as eating them!

1 cup white glutinous rice
¾ cup (6 fl oz) thick coconut milk
pinch of salt
1 tablespoon white sugar
2 or 3 drops *pandan* essence
3 ripe mangoes

Mangoes with sweet rice
(Khao Niew Ma Muang)

At a certain time of the year, this combination is all the rage in Thailand. It doesn't last long, because the rice has to be young and green, the mangoes of a certain variety. When green rice is not available, sticky or glutinous rice is used, also known as sweet rice. The green colour and special flavour of the rice comes from *bai toey*, the Thai name for pandanus leaves. They are often available fresh, but the essence or paste is more convenient to use. The Malaysian name, *pandan*, is the one usually featured on the bottle.
Serves 6

Soak the rice overnight with sufficient water to cover. Drain off the water and place the rice in a heatproof bowl. Stir in the coconut milk, salt, sugar and essence. Place the bowl on a trivet in a pressure cooker with about 5 cm (2 in) water in the pan. Bring to pressure and cook at half pressure for 30 minutes.

If a pressure cooker is not available, use a large steamer, steaming for 45 minutes to 1 hour, or until the rice is very tender and all the coconut milk absorbed.

Leave to cool slightly. Take spoonfuls of the green-tinted rice and press into lightly oiled moulds, then release with a sharp tap on a hard surface; or use an ice-cream scoop. Place on serving plates. Peel and slice the mangoes and arrange beside the rice. A simple leaf-vein carving on each mango is attractive.

To slice mangoes, use a well sharpened stainless steel knife. I always cut off a small slice from the stem end because the sap found there is very irritating to sensitive throats. If the fruit is firm, peel it with a sharp knife and cut off the flesh in thick slices, one on either side of the seed. If completely ripe, as it should be, it is easier to peel by simply pulling off the skin in strips, starting at the top where the stem end has been removed.

Serve at room temperature as the flavour of mango and texture of sticky rice are best appreciated when not chilled.

1.5 litres (6 cups) water
½ cup (3 oz) sago or tapioca
1 cup (8 fl oz) water
⅓ cup (3 oz) sugar
1 tablespoon palm sugar
2 cups (16 fl oz) coconut milk
¼ teaspoon salt
3 or 4 bananas

Bananas in sago cream
(Gluay Saku Kati)

Use whichever variety of sago or tapioca you prefer. If using the instant or quick-cooking variety, follow the instructions on package.
Serves 4

In a large saucepan bring the 1.5 litres of water to a boil and sprinkle in the sago or tapioca. Boil for 7 minutes for small grains, or 15 minutes for large tapioca. Turn off the heat, cover with a tightly fitting lid and allow to stand for a further 10–15 minutes. By this time, the grains should be perfectly clear. Run cold water into the pan and strain through a fine sieve. Hold the sieve under the cold tap to rinse excess starch away.

Combine 1 cup (8 fl oz) water with the sugar and palm sugar and stir until boiling. Simmer for 5 minutes, then stir in the coconut milk and salt. Remove from the heat and stir in the sago or tapioca.

Peel the bananas and slice thickly, holding the knife at a slight angle. In each bowl put a few slices of banana and ladle the coconut milk and sago mixture over. Serve warm or at room temperature.

Thai Desserts and Sweet Snacks

Steamed custard in pumpkin shell

(Sankaya Fug Tong)

The sweetness of pumpkin goes well with the flavour of palm sugar.
If you have difficulty buying palm sugar, use brown sugar.
Serves 4–6

200 g (6½ oz) palm sugar

¼ cup (2 fl oz) water

1¼ cups (10 fl oz) canned coconut cream

3 whole eggs

2 egg yolks

⅛ teaspoon salt

a few drops rosewater or rose essence

4–6 small golden nugget pumpkins, or 1 medium-sized pumpkin

Put the palm sugar into a small saucepan with the water. Heat gently until melted. Remove from the heat and mix with the coconut cream. Beat the eggs and egg yolks together, add to the coconut milk mixture and flavour with salt and rose flavouring. Strain into a jug.

Cut a slice off the top of each pumpkin and set aside. Scoop out all the seeds and membranes and place the pumpkins in a large steamer or on a rack in a large pan over hot water.

Fill with the custard and steam over gently boiling water for 20 minutes, or until the custard is set and a knife inserted in the centre comes out clean. Set the lids alongside the pumpkins to steam so they too will be cooked. Allow to cool, then chill. Place a lid on each pumpkin before serving.

Note:
If using one medium-to-large pumpkin instead of individual ones, the dessert is cut into wedges so each person gets a slice of pumpkin with the firm custard inside.

Caramel cups

(Khanom Tuay Fug Tong)

The little cups used for steaming these and other sweets are generally to be found in Asian stores where Thai and Vietnamese goods are sold, and are quite inexpensive.
Makes about 36

¾ cup (6 oz) palm sugar

¾ cup (6 fl oz) water

1 cup (4 oz) rice flour

3 tablespoons arrowroot

2½ cups (20 fl oz) thick coconut milk

Topping:

¼ cup (2 fl oz) thick coconut milk

1 teaspoon rice flour

¼ teaspoon salt

Caramelise the palm sugar to a dark brown colour in a wok or heavy saucepan, stirring constantly to prevent burning. Remove from the heat and add the water to dissolve the caramel. Cool and strain the syrup.

Combine the rice flour and arrowroot with ¾ cup (6 fl oz) of the coconut milk, beat well until smooth, then add the remaining coconut milk. Gradually beat in the caramel syrup.

Heat ungreased china cups for 10 minutes in a steamer and then fill with the caramel mixture. Steam for 25 minutes or until firm.

Make the topping by heating the coconut milk, rice flour and salt in a small saucepan, stirring, until it boils and thickens. Allow to cool. When the caramel cups are at room temperature, pipe on small rosettes of coconut topping to decorate. They may be served in the cups or turned out onto plates.

1½ cups split mung beans	
1 cup (8 oz) sugar	
½ cup (4 fl oz) thick coconut milk	
a few drops of jasmine essence	
food colouring	

Glazing and finishing:

3 teaspoons agar-agar powder	
2 cups (16 fl oz) water	
calyxes and stems from fresh chillies and strawberries	

Miniature moulded fruits
(Lug Chup)

The Thai name for these tiny fruits is *Lug Chup* ('u' as in 'put'), which translates as 'small magic'. They are made with mung bean paste, the Asian substitute for marzipan. It has a similar texture, but is usually flavoured with coconut milk and floral essences and keeps well in the refrigerator for at least a week. Buy the skinned and split beans, not the whole mung beans in their green skins.

Wash the beans and soak in plenty of cold water. Drain and rinse. Put them into a saucepan with just enough water to cover and cook with a lid on the pan until the beans are soft enough to mash easily between the fingers. Drain away any remaining water.

Mash the beans until smooth and return to the pan (use a heavy-based pan) with the sugar and coconut milk. Cook over medium heat, stirring constantly, for about 30 minutes. Turn the heat low as the mixture becomes drier and be careful not to let the paste catch on the base of the pan. When ready it should be very smooth and of a moulding consistency.

Remove from the heat and when cool mix in the jasmine essence. Alternatively, after the fruits are moulded and painted, store them overnight in a container with some jasmine blossoms or a scented candle to impart a faint perfume.

Take half-teaspoons of the mixture and roll into smooth balls, then mould each one to represent a fruit or vegetable in miniature. Insert a fine toothpick in the stem end of each fruit, then paint them with food colouring and stick the other end into a block of polystyrene while they dry.

Prepare the glaze, dip each fruit and once again leave to dry on the toothpick. When all the fruit have been dipped, start with those fruits which were done first and dip them all a second time. This gives a very smooth and shiny glaze. When all the fruit are quite dry and no longer sticky to the touch, remove the toothpicks. Insert tiny leaves made by trimming to size twigs of murraya or other non-toxic plant varieties. Calyxes from fresh chillies or strawberries are also used to give a life-like appearance to the moulded fruits. Serve as part of a selection of sweets at the end of a meal.

Glaze:
Sprinkle the agar-agar powder over the water and heat gently until it is completely dissolved. Allow to cool slightly before dipping the fruits. Because agar-agar sets at room temperature, it will be necessary to reheat it gently to keep it at a liquid consistency.

An alternative glaze can be made from 2 tablespoons gelatine dissolved in 2 cups (16 fl oz) water. Sprinkle the gelatine over 1 cup (8 fl oz) water and leave to soak for 5 minutes, then dissolve it – either in the microwave oven (on HIGH for 35–40 seconds), or by standing the cup in a small pan of simmering water on the stove. When the gelatine is quite dissolved allow it to cool to room temperature and stir in the remaining cup of water which should also be at the same temperature. This solution may be cooled more than the agar-agar because it will not set as readily, and will not need to be melted as many times.

Note:
The moulded fruits in the photograph were made by my daughter Nina. She says she learned from me, but her results are undeniably better than anything I can achieve.

Thai Desserts and Sweet Snacks

16 pieces of banana leaf, or thick foil, 18 cm (7 in) square
¼ cup (2 oz) white sugar
½ teaspoon salt
1 cup (8 fl oz) coconut milk
1 cup white glutinous rice, washed and soaked overnight
3 bananas
¼ cup dried black beans, cooked (yields 1 cup cooked beans)

Dough:

1½ cups glutinous rice flour
½ cup (4 fl oz) boiling water

Filling:

½ cup dried mung beans without skin
1 tablespoon sugar
2 tablespoons finely grated coconut
½ teaspoon salt

Coating:

1½ cups finely grated fresh coconut
¼ cup toasted, crushed sesame seeds
¼ cup (2 oz) caster (superfine) sugar

Steamed glutinous rice with banana, Mock bean pods

Steamed glutinous rice with banana
(Khao Tom Phad)
Makes about 16

Strip the banana leaves from their mid-ribs and wash them well. Tear into 18 cm (7 in) pieces and, holding each piece with tongs, pass them briefly over a gas flame to make them pliable. Whether using banana leaves or foil, make a small pleat 1.25 cm (½ in) wide down the centre of each piece to allow for the rice swelling during cooking.

Mix the sugar and salt with the coconut milk, add the drained rice and stir over moderate heat until the coconut milk is absorbed. The rice will still be only partially cooked.

Place 1 tablespoon of rice in the centre of each piece of leaf or foil. Cover with sliced banana and top with another tablespoon of rice. Press 6 black beans into the rice. Wrap and tie the leaf or fasten the folded ends with wooden toothpicks. If using foil, make a narrow double fold over the top of the rice and fold in the ends to seal. Repeat until all the rice is used up. Steam over boiling water for 45–50 minutes.

Note:
To cook black beans, wash them to remove any dust, then cover with water and bring to the boil. Put the lid on the pan and leave to stand for 1 hour. Return to the heat and simmer for 30–40 minutes, or until tender. Leftover beans may be frozen for future use.

Mock bean pods
(Khanom Tuay Paep)
Makes about 24

Dough:
Sift the flour into a bowl and gradually add the water to form a soft dough. When cool enough knead until smooth. Divide the dough in half and roll each piece into a cylinder 2.5 cm (1 in) in diameter, then cut into 2.5 cm (1 in) slices. Keep the working surface dusted with extra glutinous rice flour and roll each piece into a ball. Cover these with a dry cloth and set aside.

Filling:
Cook the beans in boiling water to cover for about 10 minutes or until they are soft but not broken. Drain well, add the sugar and stir over low heat 5–10 minutes longer. Mash lightly and mix with the grated coconut and salt.

With floured fingers, flatten each ball of dough to a circle 6 cm (2½ in) in diameter and place 1 teaspoonful of filling in the centre. Pinch the edges together firmly, then soften the pinched edge and round it off to look like a seed pod. Continue with the remaining dough and filling.

Drop the 'pods' into boiling water and when they float, lift them out on a slotted spoon and drain. Toss them in the grated coconut and sprinkle liberally with the sesame seeds and caster sugar mixed together.

Do not refrigerate, and serve on the same day.

2 cups white glutinous rice
1½ cups (12 fl oz) thick coconut milk
3 pinches of salt
3 tablespoons white sugar
red and green food colouring
2 or 3 drops each *pandan* (*bai toey*), rose and jasmine essences
about 1 cup grated fresh coconut

Sticky rice balls in fresh coconut
(Khao Niew Kluk Maprao)

Many Thai sweets are based on glutinous rice which clings together most conveniently. Here the rice is flavoured and coloured before cooking, then rolled into oval shapes and coated with fresh coconut. For ways to grate coconut, *see page 13.*
Serves 6

Soak the rice overnight with sufficient water to cover. Drain off the water and divide the rice and coconut milk equally between 3 heatproof bowls. Stir a pinch of salt and tablespoon of sugar into each bowl.

To one bowl add a drop or two of green food colouring and the *pandan* essence. To the second, add a drop or two of red food colouring – just enough to give a pale pink shade – and flavour with rose essence. To the third bowl add some jasmine essence. Place the bowls in a steamer over hot water and bring to the boil. Cover and steam for 45 minutes to 1 hour, until the rice is very tender and all the coconut milk absorbed.

Leave to cool slightly, then take spoonfuls of rice and roll into even-sized balls or ovals. Roll in grated fresh coconut and arrange on a plate.

These lightly sweetened snacks should not be refrigerated, but eaten the same day.

2 tablespoons mung bean flour
2 cups (16 fl oz) water
¾ cup (6 oz) sugar
jasmine essence
food colouring (optional)

Topping:

¼ cup (2 fl oz) coconut milk
1 teaspoon rice flour
pinch of salt

'Forget to swallow'
(Khanom Lüm Klün)

This is the literal translation of the Thai name for these simple but delicious sweets, translucent, and so tender that they slip down without any effort.
Makes about 24

Combine the mung bean flour, water and sugar in a saucepan, stirring until the flour is evenly distributed. Place over medium heat and bring to the boil, stirring constantly. If you like, divide the mixture in two or three portions and colour each one a delicate shade with one or two drops of food colouring.

Have ready little foil or waxed paper confectionery cups or, if possible, small square boxes made from fresh *pandan* (*bai toey*) leaves. Pour a little of the mixture into each cup and leave to set.

Heat the coconut milk, rice flour and salt together until it boils and thickens, then leave to cool. Put into a piping bag fitted with a star or flower nozzle, and pipe a tiny shape onto each sweet. The slightly salty taste of the coconut contrasts delightfully with the sweets.

Sticky rice balls in fresh coconut

1 cup (4 oz) rice flour
1 tablespoon arrowroot
½ cup (4 oz) sugar
2 cups (16 fl oz) water, flavoured with jasmine
green and pink food colouring

Dimpled cups
(Khanom Nam Dog Mai)
Makes about 18

Combine the rice flour and arrowroot. Heat the sugar and 1 cup
(8 fl oz) water together in a pan, stirring to dissolve the sugar. Mix
into the flour and knead well until smooth. Gradually add the
remaining cup of water.

Place small china cups in a steamer and steam for 10 minutes to
heat. Divide the mixture in half and add a drop or two of green or
pink food colouring to each. While the cups are hot, fill them three-
quarters full with the mixture and steam for 20–25 minutes over
boiling water, until the surface is dimpled and firm. Serve warm or
at room temperature.

*Dimpled cups, "Forget to
swallow",Layered sweet,
Caramel cups, Coconut
icecream*

1 x 400 ml (13 fl oz) can coconut milk
100 ml (3½ fl oz) sweetened condensed milk
¾ cup (6 fl oz) water
⅓ cup (3 oz) sugar
1½ teaspoons gelatine
¼ cup (2 fl oz) cold water

Note:
Another very effective way to smooth out ice crystals when making ice-cream without a churn is to let the mixture freeze solid, then break it up into chunks and purée in a food processor until smooth. Return it to the tray and refreeze.

Coconut ice-cream

(I-Tim Kati)

When I think of coconut ice-cream, I am whisked back in time to a memorable evening at the famous Oriental Hotel in Bangkok. Under a full moon, the *Loy Krathong* Festival was celebrated with tableaux and Thai classical dancing and much festivity. At the end of an incredible buffet meal, the chef appeared with coconut ice-cream so fresh it was still in its churn, and served it to the appreciative guests.
Serves 6

Combine the coconut milk and condensed milk in a bowl. Put ¾ cup (6 fl oz) water and the sugar in a small saucepan and heat gently, stirring until sugar dissolves. Sprinkle the gelatine over ¼ cup (2 fl oz) cold water and leave to soften for a few minutes, then stir into the hot syrup. Cool the syrup, add to the coconut milk mixture and freeze the mixture in an ice-cream churn.

Alternatively, freeze in a shallow tray and when it is frozen around the edges but still slushy in the centre, turn it into a chilled bowl and whisk until smooth but not melted. Return it to the tray and freeze until firm. Leave at room temperature for a few minutes before serving. Decorate with shreds of toasted coconut or with very fine strips of agar-agar jelly (*page 194*). Pour some liquid jelly on a dinner plate to form a shallow layer. When set, cut with a sharp knife.

1 cup black glutinous rice
cold water
¼ teaspoon salt
1 cup freshly grated coconut
2 tablespoons sesame seeds
extra ½ teaspoon sea salt
4 tablespoons palm sugar or dark brown sugar

Black sticky rice
(Khao Niew Dum)

The best results, I feel, are obtained when the rice is soaked overnight, then steamed in a pressure cooker or steamer.
Serves 4

Wash the rice well and soak it overnight in cold water. Drain the rice and place in a heatproof bowl with ¾ cup (6 fl oz) of the soaking water. Steam as described in Mangoes with Sweet Rice (*page 182*).

While the rice steams, grate the coconut and toast the sesame seeds. To grate coconut, try and use a grater designed specifically for the purpose (*see* Implements, *page 24*). Toast the sesame seeds in a dry frying pan over medium heat, stirring or shaking the pan all the time so the seeds brown evenly. As soon as they are a deep golden colour, turn them onto a plate. Bruise lightly in a mortar together with the sea salt. Serve the rice warm or at room temperature, accompanied by the coconut, sesame seeds and palm sugar.

¾ cup (3 oz) rice flour
185 g (6 oz) *khanom chaun* flour (a mixture of rice and tapioca flour sold in packets)
280 g (9 oz) sugar
1 x 400 ml (13 fl oz) can coconut milk
½ teaspoon salt
3 cups (24 fl oz) water
pandan (bai toey) paste

Layered sweet

(Khanom Chaun)
Makes 45 or more pieces, depending on size

Mix all the ingredients together, stirring gently, until smooth. Strain through a fine sieve. Take out 1 cup (8 fl oz) of the batter and set aside. Divide the remainder into 2 equal portions. Colour one of these light green with the *pandan* paste. Leave the other portion white.

Spray a 23 cm (9 in) square tin with non-stick spray, or brush it lightly with oil. Place on a rack over hot water in an electric frypan or steamer, cover and bring to the boil (set frypan at 200°C/400°F).

Pour in a thin layer (about a scant cupful) of light green batter and steam for 5 minutes, or until set. Pour on the same amount of white batter and steam for 5 minutes. Continue in this way until the batter is used up, except for the cupful of batter which was set aside. Colour this a deep green with *pandan* paste and pour over the other layers. Steam the final layer for 15 minutes. Cool and cut into squares. Do not refrigerate, and serve these the same day.

Variation:
Instead of green and white layers, colour one portion pale pink and the other pale green. Save a cupful of caramel mixture (*see* Caramel Cups, *page 183*). Make several thin layers of each colour and cook as above.

Agar-agar jellies
(Woon)

2 cups (16 fl oz) water

2 teaspoons agar-agar powder

⅓ cup (3 oz) sugar

red, green and blue food
    colourings

rose or jasmine essence

pandan (*bai toey*) essence

1 tablespoon coconut milk, or
    evaporated milk

salt

Agar-agar is refined from seaweed and gives a clear, firm jelly which will not melt even in tropical heat. If you're ever in Thailand, go into a department store and buy some miniature jelly moulds. Otherwise, use small French tartlet moulds or foil cups for the jellies.

Makes about 30 tiny jellies

Pour the water into a saucepan and sprinkle the agar-agar powder over the surface. Bring slowly to the boil and stir until the agar-agar is completely dissolved. Add the sugar and stir until the sugar dissolves. Remove from the heat and divide between 4 bowls. Leave one portion plain. Colour and flavour the other three as desired. Into the plain portion stir the coconut milk and a tiny pinch of salt which accentuates the flavour of the coconut.

Pour into small moulds. If making more than one layer, set the moulds in the refrigerator to chill while you keep the rest of the jelly warm in a pan of simmering water. When the first layer has set, add the next. When set, slip them out of the moulds with gentle pressure on one side. Turn the shapes upside down on the serving plate. It is quite in order to pick them up with the fingers for eating.

If small moulds are not available, use tiny confectionery cups to set the jellies. If the cups are waxed paper, use two or three together for stability. Foil cups hold their shape better.

Tapioca with sweet corn and young coconut
(Saku, Khao Poad, Maprao Orn)

½ cup (3 oz) tapioca

¾ cup (6 fl oz) water

3 tablespoons sugar

½ cup sweet corn kernels

½ cup young coconut, cut
    neatly into squares or
    diamond shapes

Those who have encountered young coconut in lands where it grows will know that the flesh of an immature nut is quite different from the hard white meat of a mature coconut. At this stage of development the meat is soft and sweet. Translucent at first, it becomes slightly milky in appearance, yet is soft enough to spoon from the shell. This young coconut is now available either frozen or in cans.

Serves 4

Cook the tapioca as described in the recipe for Bananas in Sago Cream, (*page 182*). Drain and rinse.

Make a syrup with the water and sugar boiled together for 3 minutes. Add the corn kernels and simmer gently for about 10 minutes, adding more water if the syrup boils down and becomes thick – this should be a light syrup. Cool to room temperature.

Combine the tapioca and syrup, then stir in the young coconut. Divide between 4 bowls and serve warm.

Agar agar jellies

Yellow mixture:

1 cup glutinous rice flour

1 cup steamed, mashed
pumpkin

White mixture:

1 cup glutinous rice flour

1 cup cooked, mashed and
sieved potato or taro

Green mixture:

1 cup glutinous rice flour

bai toey leaves or essence

Coconut syrup:

2 cups (16 fl oz) coconut milk

½ cup (4 oz) white sugar, or
to taste

¼ teaspoon salt

Three-coloured sweet rice balls
(Bua Loy Sarm See)

When in Thailand researching this book, one of my priorities was to learn how to make the fascinating sweets. I could hardly believe my eyes when I found out that each of the tiny little balls of rice flour in this dessert is moulded by hand! Yet, if two or three friends sit together and the talk is entertaining, it is done in half an hour, most pleasantly.
Serves 6–8

In three separate bowls make mixtures of the rice flour with the mashed vegetables and, in the case of the third mixture, with sufficient water to moisten and make a firm dough. Add a few drops of cold water if the mixtures are too stiff, a little extra rice flour if too soft to hold their shape when moulded.

Take tiny bits of the dough and form smooth balls, keeping each colour separate. Bring a pan of water to the boil and cook one colour at a time, simmering, until they come to the surface. Lift out on a wire spoon and put into separate bowls of iced water.

Combine the coconut milk, sugar and salt in a saucepan and stir while bringing to the boil. Remove from heat and cool until just warm. For each serving, place ½ cup of the rice balls, in a mixture of colours, in each bowl with enough milk to cover, and serve warm or at room temperature.

Note:
If only a small amount of dessert is needed, halve these quantities. You can, in fact, use half the white mixture, flavoured and coloured a delicate green with *pandan* essence to replace the full quantity of green mixture.

Water chestnut sweet, Three-coloured sweet balls, Basil seeds in coconut syrup, Tapioca with sweet corn and young coconut

¾ cup (6 oz) sugar
¾ cup (6 fl oz) water
200 g (7 oz) water chestnuts, fresh or canned
red food colouring
rosewater or jasmine essence
green food colouring
a few drops *pandan* essence
about ¾ cup (5 oz) tapioca flour
1 cup (8 fl oz) fresh coconut milk
⅛ teaspoon salt
crushed ice

Water chestnut sweet
(Tuptim Grob)

Tuptim means 'rubies', and it is also the word for pomegranate; *grob* means 'crisp, crunchy'. A descriptive name for this simple dessert based on little pieces of water chestnuts with a glistening, transparent coating of tapioca flour. Fresh coconut milk is really superior to canned coconut milk in desserts, and should be used if fresh coconuts are available.
Serves 4

Make a syrup with the sugar and water, stirring over heat until the sugar dissolves. Cool.

Drain the canned water chestnuts, rinse in cold water, then cut each one into about 8 pieces, roughly equal in size. If fresh water chestnuts are available, peel, dice and boil them for 10 minutes.

Pour ½ cup (4 fl oz) water into each of two white bowls. Add red food colouring and a few drops of rose or jasmine essence to one, and green food colouring and *pandan* essence to the other. Make the colours fairly strong. Add half the diced water chestnuts to one bowl and half to the other, stir and leave to soak for 10 minutes.

Divide the tapioca flour between two sheets of greaseproof (non-stick baking) paper. Drain the soaking water chestnuts if they have absorbed a fair amount of colour, otherwise leave them longer. Roll them in the tapioca flour until well coated, and keep the two colours separate.

Bring a saucepan of water to the boil. Gently shake the red-tinted water chestnuts in a strainer, or toss from hand to hand so excess flour comes away. Drop into the boiling water and allow to cook until the pieces rise to the surface. Drain and plunge immediately into iced water.

Using fresh boiling water, repeat the procedure with the green-tinted chestnuts, and cool them in a separate bowl of iced water.

To serve, pour a quarter of the syrup into a tall glass and carefully place some green, then some red-tinted chestnuts in the glass, keeping the layers separate. Gently spoon over some of the coconut milk mixed with the salt, and add crushed ice. Or serve in bowls as shown in the photograph on *page 196*.

2 tablespoons basil (*manglak*) seeds
2 cups (16 fl oz) coconut milk
½ cup (4 oz) sugar
½ cup glutinous rice flour
blue food colouring
a few drops jasmine or rose essence

Basil seeds in coconut syrup
(Med Manglak Nam Kati)

Serves 4

Soak the basil seeds in a bowl of water for 10 minutes, until each black seed develops a jelly-like translucent coating. Warm the coconut milk and dissolve the sugar in it.

Mix the rice flour with just enough cold water to give a moulding consistency and work in a drop or two of blue food colouring to give a delicate shade. Take small pieces and roll between the palms to make little 'snake' shapes. Drop into a pan of boiling water and when they float to the top, lift them out on a slotted spoon and immerse in a bowl of iced water.

At serving time combine the soaked seeds and the sweetened coconut milk. Drain the blue rice flour shapes and stir in. If you like, add a little crushed ice.

Gold layer:

½ cup split and skinned mung beans

½ cup (4 oz) sugar

1 cup (8 fl oz) coconut milk

¼ teaspoon jasmine essence

¼ teaspoon yellow food colouring

½ cup glutinous rice flour

¼ cup tapioca flour

Green layer:

½ cup tapioca flour

2 tablespoons glutinous rice flour

1 cup (8 fl oz) water

⅓ cup (3 oz) sugar

½ teaspoon *pandan* (*bai toey*) paste or essence (for colour and flavour), or green food colouring

Green and gold layered pudding
(Khanom Chaun Tua)

The gold layer is made with mung bean paste, sweetened and flavoured with coconut milk, while the clear green layer is tapioca starch. They are poured into a pan and steamed in layers and the final result is a pretty ribbon effect of contrasting colours and textures.
Makes about 30 pieces

Wash the mung beans and put them into a small pan with water to cover. Boil gently for about 15–20 minutes, or until they are very soft, then drain off any water which has not been absorbed. Mash with a fork or potato masher until smooth.

Add the sugar and coconut milk and mix well, then stir in the jasmine essence, yellow food colouring, rice flour and tapioca flour.

Spray a 20–23 cm (8–9 in) round or square pan with non-stick food spray, or brush lightly with tasteless salad oil. Pour in one-third of the mixture and place in a bamboo basket. Cover and steam for 5–8 minutes over boiling water, until set.

Meanwhile, make the green layer, mixing together both kinds of flour, the water and sugar. Colour a deep green and flavour with *pandan* paste or essence. Pour half the green mixture over the first layer, cover and steam for 10 minutes, or until firm. There may be a little liquid on the surface, so pick up the pan using a tea towel or heatproof mitts and pour it off.

Gently ladle another third of the gold mixture over the green layer, add more boiling water if necessary, and steam a further 5–8 minutes until firm. Repeat with the remaining green mixture as before, and finally the last of the gold mixture. Steam for 10 minutes, then leave to become quite cold.

Cut into strips, squares or diamond shapes. This sweet may be made ahead and kept refrigerated for a few days.

½ cup (4 oz) sugar

2 tablespoons palm sugar, optional

1 cup (8 fl oz) water

3 cups (24 fl oz) fresh coconut milk, or 2 cups (16 fl oz) canned coconut milk and 1 cup (8 fl oz) water

1 cup tender corn kernels sliced from the cob, or drained canned corn

3 or 4 ripe bananas, cut into chunks

2 drops jasmine essence

1 tablespoon toasted sesame seeds (optional)

Bananas in coconut cream
(Gluay Khao Poad Gaeng Buad)

Many Asian desserts are fairly liquid mixtures and this is one of the most popular.
Serves 4–6

Make a syrup with the sugar, palm sugar and water. Add the coconut milk, corn and bananas and simmer uncovered for 5 minutes. Remove from the heat and cool to lukewarm. Stir in the jasmine essence and spoon into bowls. Serve slightly warm or at room temperature, with a sprinkling of toasted sesame seeds if desired.

Pumpkin layer:

1 cup cooked, mashed pumpkin

1 cup tapioca flour

¼ cup (2 oz) sugar

¼ cup (2 fl oz) water

Coconut layer:

½ cup (4 fl oz) thick coconut milk

1 teaspoon rice flour (not glutinous)

¼ teaspoon salt

---

500 g (1 lb) pumpkin, cooked and mashed

1¼ cups (10 fl oz) coconut milk

¾ cup (6 oz) sugar

½ teaspoon jasmine essence

1 cup (4 oz) rice flour

¼ cup tapioca flour

¾ teapoon salt

1 cup freshly grated coconut

extra grated coconut mixed with a pinch of salt, (optional)

---

3 or 4 ladies' finger bananas

2 cups (16 fl oz) coconut milk

4 tablespoons sugar

pinch of salt

Steamed pumpkin pudding,
Two-layered pumpkin puddings

Two-layer pumpkin puddings
(Khanom Tuay)

Makes about 15

In a bowl combine the pumpkin, tapioca flour, sugar and water, mixing well until the sugar dissolves. Lightly oil small china cups (wine cups or other similar sized heatproof cups), with tasteless salad oil and three-quarters fill with the pumpkin mixture. Place in a steamer and steam over boiling water for 20 minutes.

Turn off the heat but do not remove the cups from the steamer. Mix together the coconut milk, rice flour and salt, and pour a teaspoonful over the top of each little pudding. Add more water if necessary and steam for a further 10 minutes. Cool, then run a knife around the edge, unmould and serve at room temperature. Do not chill.

Steamed pumpkin pudding
(Khanom Fug Tong)

Makes about 25 pieces

Lightly brush a 20 cm (8 in) square or round tin with tasteless salad oil. Sieve the pumpkin, or purée in a food processor. Warm the coconut milk and stir in the sugar until dissolved. Combine the coconut milk and pumpkin, and flavour with jasmine essence.

Sift both kinds of flour and ½ teaspoon salt into a bowl, then mix in the pumpkin mixture and ½ cup of the grated coconut. Pour into the prepared tin and sprinkle with the remaining coconut mixed with the remaining ¼ teaspoon salt. Place the tin in a steamer and steam over fast boiling water for 30–35 minutes, or until firm. Allow to cool, then cut into squares or diamond shapes with a wet knife. Sprinkle with additional lightly salted coconut if desired.

Bananas in sweet coconut milk
(Gluay Buad Chee)

Simple to make, this is one of the more popular desserts served in restaurants.
Serves 4

Peel the bananas and cut into bite-sized pieces. Dilute the coconut milk if using the canned variety and put into a saucepan with the sugar and salt. Stir until boiling, then boil for 2 minutes.

Add the banana pieces and simmer over low heat for 2 minutes, or until the bananas are soft but still retain their shape. They may be cooked longer if a softer result is preferred, but they do lose texture. Serve warm.

Glossary

Thanks to the popularity of Thai food worldwide, many food companies in Thailand are exporting an excellent range of spices, sauces, herbs, and other requisites.

A few years ago galangal was only sold dried, in slices or ground, but it is now available fresh-frozen or bottled in brine. I have even been able to buy the whole, fresh rhizome. I planted it and, since it grows vigorously, can now use it from my own garden. Lemon grass is becoming quite common, and suburban Asian grocery stores more often than not sell bundles of fresh lemon grass.

Ingredients are obviously best if used in their fresh form, but since not everybody has access to large Asian shopping centres, I have also listed other forms in which they are sold. Bearing in mind that demand creates a supply, keep asking your local supplier for what you need and undoubtedly it will become available.

Agar-Agar

Thai: *Woon*

This setting agent refined from seaweed is sometimes known as vegetable gelatine. The advantage is that it sets and stays solid without refrigeration and is therefore ideal for using in warm climates. It may be bought in powder form or strands at Asian grocery stores, some health food stores and chemists. Gelatine is not really a suitable substitute as the texture will be totally different and it will take twice as much gelatine powder to set the given amount of liquid.

Steamed dumplings

Basil

Thai: *Horapa; manglak; krapow*
Bot: *Ocimum basilicum; ocimum canum; ocimum sanctum*
Fam: *Labiatae*

Basil is an important herb in Thai cooking and the three names refer to three varieties. Dried basil would be a poor substitute. Since basil is easily grown, it is worth keeping a few plants of sweet basil in a pot or window box.

Horapa is the most commonly used and is equivalent to the large-leaf sweet basil (*Ocimum basilicum*) best known in European cooking.

The smaller leaf of *manglak* (*ocimum canum*) is more pungent and lemon scented, and its seeds (*luk manglak*) are used in desserts and drinks. They are supposed to have a cooling effect on the body, and are used as a medicine for stomach ailments. When dry they are tiny, oval and brownish-black. When soaked in cold water for a few minutes, they develop a slippery, translucent coat around the seed, which is why they are sometimes called 'frog's eggs'.

The third kind of basil, *krapow* (*ocimum sanctum*), is used only in curries. Its leaves are tinged with red.

Bean Curd

Thai: *Tao hu*

Made from soy beans, bean curd takes many forms. There is the soft, fresh bean curd used in soups and other dishes, usually sold in a container with water which should be changed daily for the 2 or 3 days it will keep in the refrigerator. If you wish to keep bean curd for some time, it is better to buy Japanese tofu in sealed packages which keeps for months without refrigeration. After opening store in the refrigerator and use within 2 days. Freezing is not recommended.

Pressed or firm bean curd is sold in blocks, wrapped in plastic film. It is used in fried dishes as it is less likely to disintegrate during cooking. One thing I have learned is that it generally does not keep quite as long as the date on the package states, so use it fairly promptly or it will become discoloured and develop a slimy surface and sour smell.

Fermented or red bean curd (sold in jars) is sometimes added to sauces. It keeps well and imparts a salty, pungent flavour.

Bean curd skin is sold dried, the fine sheets folded flat. Soak in warm water until flexible before using it to wrap certain foods.

Bean Starch Vermicelli

Thai: *Woon sen*

Also known as cellophane noodles or jelly noodles, these fine, transparent noodles are made from the starch of green mung beans. In some recipes they are soaked in hot water before use, in others they are dropped into boiling water and cooked until tender. It requires considerable effort to cut through the threads when they are dry, so I recommend buying small bundles rather than the large ones which need dividing. These noodles will keep indefinitely.

Bitter Gourd

Thai: *Ma ra*
Bot: *Momordica charantia*

A gourd with a distinctive bitter flavour which is probably an
acquired taste. It resembles a green cucumber pointed at the tip and
with a glossy, pebbly-textured skin. Dark green when immature, it
turns golden with red seeds when ripe, but the time to use it is when
it is apple green and the seeds are still pale and tender. No
substitute.

Black Fungus

Thai: *Hed hunu*
Bot: *Auricularia polytricha*

Also known as 'jelly mushrooms' or 'cloud ear fungus', it is sold in
dried form and resembles greyish-black bits of torn paper. When
soaked in water for 10 minutes it swells to translucent, jelly-like
brown shapes from which it gets its descriptive names. Having no
flavour of its own, it is used for its resilient texture and testifies to
the Chinese influence in Thai cooking. It may be omitted without
affecting the dish.

Black Sticky Rice

Thai: *Khao niew*

This glutinous rice is used in sweets and has a chewy texture which
is very pleasant.

Cardamom

Thai: *Luk kravan*
Bot: *Elettaria cardamomum*
Fam: *Zingiberaceae*

This fragrant spice is not typically found in Thai dishes, but is an
important part of Masaman curry which is a favourite Indian-influenced
Thai dish.

Cha Plu

Bot: *Piper sarmentosum*

A creeper belonging to the pepper family, this plant has no
English name that I can trace. It has glossy green leaves
with a spiciness reminiscent of betel leaves, and is used
to enclose little snacks so it forms an edible wrapping.
Substitute soft lettuce or tender spinach leaves.

Chillies

Thai: *Prik*
Bot: *Capsicum frutescens*
Fam: *Solanaceae*

Chillies come in all sizes and a variety of shapes and colours. Fresh chillies used in Thai cooking are usually the small, hot ones. As a general rule, large chillies are milder and the tiny ones are devilishly hot. Colour is no indication, because I have tasted yellow chillies which should have been red for danger! So if very hot food is not to your taste, use larger chillies for flavour without excessive heat. Please refer to the precautions for handling chillies in the section on Curry Pastes on *page 18*. Dried chillies are safer to handle, but wash your hands well afterwards.

Dried chillies are also sold as coarse flakes or fine powder. Flakes are more often used in Thai food.

Cinnamon

Thai: *Ob chuey*
Bot: *Cinnamomum zeylanicum*
Fam: *Lauraceae*

This is not much used in Thai food except in dishes with an Indian influence such as Masaman curry. You can distinguish true cinnamon by the thin, pale bark which is sun-dried to form quills packed one inside the other. Buy the quills because most of what is sold as ground cinnamon is actually ground cassia – similar in flavour, but much stronger and lacking the delicacy of true cinnamon.

Coconut Milk, Fresh Grated Coconut Desiccated Coconut *(page 12)*

Coriander (Cilantro/Chinese parsley)

Thai: *Pak chee*
Bot: *Coriandrum sativum*
Fam: *Umbelliferae*

Fresh coriander herb is one of the indispensable ingredients in Thai cooking. It is generally readily available in large fruit and vegetable markets, and most certainly in Asian stores. But if you don't live within reach of these facilities, it is not difficult to grow the herb – all you need is a patch of earth and patience, since the seeds take from 18–21 days to germinate. Scatter the seeds, cover very lightly with soil and water regularly.

The distinctive, pungent flavour of coriander does not survive in dried form. If fresh coriander is not available, substitute fresh mint or fresh sweet basil. The flavour will be different, but preferable to dried coriander leaves.

Coriander seeds, on the other hand, are used dried. They are sold whole or ground, and are a basic ingredient in curry pastes. The aroma and flavour are quite different to that of the fresh herb.

Cummin

Thai: *Yee ra*
Bot: *Cuminum cyminum*
Fam: *Umbelliferae*

An important component of curry pastes, cummin may be bought as whole seeds or ground. Before using, roast lightly until fragrant. The best results come from buying the whole seeds, roasting and pounding them finely with a mortar and pestle, or using an efficient spice grinder.

Dried Shrimp (*see* Shrimp, Dried)

Eggplant (Aubergine)

Thai: *Makua*

Bot: *Solanum*

A very popular vegetable in Thailand, and there are many varieties used, from small, green and pea-sized to the large purple or white. In between there are eggplants about the size and shape of eggs (perhaps this is what led to its English name). The skins of some have a delicate green and white tracery, while others are in pretty mauve shades. These are sometimes eaten raw with a *Nam Prik* sauce.

Fish Sauce

Thai: *Nam pla*

This thin, brown, salty sauce is made from a small variety of fish or from tiny shrimp which are layered with salt and left in the sun. The salty liquid drips through into a container, is bottled, and then left in the sun until it is clear and pale and has developed its characteristic smell. Mixed with lime juice or chillies, it is used as a condiment in Thailand, besides being an indispensable ingredient in cooking.

Galangal (Greater)

Thai: *Kha*
Bot: *Alpinia galanga*
Fam: *Zingiberaceae*

This is greater galangal, a rhizome which looks similar to ginger and is sometimes called Siamese Ginger. Until Thai food became so popular, it was mostly labelled with its Indonesian name of *Laos* or its Malaysian name, *Lengkuas*. It is sold in many forms – fresh, frozen, bottled in brine, sliced and dried, or dried and ground. Wherever possible use fresh, frozen or bottled galangal.

Galangal (Lesser)

Thai: *Krachai*
Bot: *Kaempferia pandurata*
Fam: *Zingiberaceae*

The slender tubers of the lesser galangal grow in a bunch and look nothing at all like ginger. They are smaller but more strongly flavoured than greater galangal, and are used less frequently, mostly in fish dishes.

Garlic

Thai: *Kratiem*
Bot: *Allium sativum*
Fam: *Liliaceae*

Garlic is the indispensable ingredient in Thai cooking, and fortunately it is available everywhere in its fresh form. It is valued not only for the flavour it imparts, but also for its health-giving properties as it controls high blood pressure, reduces cholesterol and is a natural antibiotic. Since garlic cloves vary greatly in size, I have given measurements in teaspoons of finely chopped or crushed garlic.

Dried garlic is sometimes in granulated form, sometimes in thin slices or flakes. When crisp-fried garlic is needed, save time and effort by using dried garlic flakes. Just be aware that they cook very quickly and must not be allowed to brown or they will become bitter. To lift them quickly from the oil all at once, a fine wire strainer is invaluable. When fried and cooled, crush them for sprinkling over appetisers or salads.

Pickled garlic (*kratiem dong*) is another popular flavour accent in Thai dishes such as the famous *Mee Grob* (Crispy Fried Noodles). Sold in jars in a light pickling mixture of vinegar, sugar and salt, it will keep indefinitely without refrigeration. Do not attempt to separate or peel the cloves, simply slice through the whole bulb.

Garlic Chives

Thai: *Ton kui chai*
Bot: *Allium tuberosum*
Fam: *Liliaceae*

Also known as Chinese chives, these flat, thick leaves are served alongside noodle dishes, or cut into short lengths and added.

Ginger

Thai: *Khing*
Bot: *Zingiber officinale*
Fam: *Zingiberaceae*

Whenever ginger is mentioned in Thai recipes, it is the fresh rhizome which is meant, not dried, ground ginger. The two are not interchangeable. To preserve fresh ginger it can be (1) cut into pieces, wrapped in foil and frozen; (2) peeled, divided into small pieces and packed in a well washed and dried bottle covered with dry sherry; (3) puréed in a blender with just enough water and dry sherry to facilitate movement, then stored in a glass screwtop jar in the refrigerator. It will keep for a few weeks and is convenient to spoon out as required. Fresh minced ginger can also be bought in supermarkets.

The strength of ginger depends on how mature it is, and if a recipe asks for a large amount it is best to try and get young, tender and pink-tipped ginger. Or follow the instructions given in individual recipes on how to lessen its impact. If ginger is young and tender it doesn't need peeling but if mature and thick-skinned, scrape off the skin with a sharp knife. Chop finely or grate before measuring, discarding any tough fibres that collect on the grater.

Green Pawpaw (Papaya)

Thai: *Malakaw*
Bot: *Carica papaya*

Unripe pawpaws are used to make a very popular *yum* or salad called *Som Tam*. Some shops or stalls sell only this item.

Golden Mountain Sauce

Thai: *Poo kow tong*

This clear brown salty sauce looks like light soy sauce or fish sauce, but tastes like neither. The nearest equivalent is a Swiss product called Maggi Seasoning or, in Europe, Maggi Arome – a well established product of which, I do believe, the Golden Mountain Sauce is a copy . . . even the bottle and label look similar. It is based on hydrolysed vegetable proteins and certainly gives a lift to flavours.

Jasmine

Thai: *Mali*
Bot: *Jasminum sambac*

The unopened flower buds are picked in the cool of the evening and soaked in water overnight to impart their fragrance. This water is used for making sweets, sometimes for extracting the coconut milk to be used in desserts. Jasmine essence (labelled *Mali*) is available, and probably more practical even if not quite as romantic.

Kaffir Lime

Thai: *Makrut*
Bot: *Citrus hystrix*
Fam: *Rutaceae*

The leaves and rind of this lumpy-skinned green lime add a special fragrance to Thai food. Try and cultivate a Thai friend who will probably have a tree in her garden! Or look for shops specialising in Thai ingredients and buy frozen or dried lime leaves. These are fine in dishes where they are simmered to impart flavour, but in salads or wherever fine shreds of the leaf are required, it is not possible to use the dried leaves, so substitute fresh lime or lemon leaves. Although the fragrance is different, in these recipes they are preferable to dried leaves.

The rind of kaffir limes is also used for an intense citrus flavour and the best way to obtain this (unless you have access to fresh limes) is to buy frozen kaffir limes which are available in plastic packets. Keep them in the freezer so they are very hard, then grate on the fine surface of a grater. Use only the coloured portion, not the white pith underneath. The rind is also sold dried, but because it has the white pith with it, it tastes rather bitter. Use it if you like, but in small quantities. A suitable alternative is the rind of fresh Tahitian or West Indian limes.

Khanom Chaun Flour

A mixture of rice flour and tapioca flour used in making sweetmeats. No substitute.

Lemon Grass

Thai: *Takrai*
Bot: *Cymbopogon citratus*
Fam: *Gramineae*

This hardy herb is easy to grow and the plants may be purchased at many nurseries. It grows throughout Asia and also in Australia, Africa, South America and Florida in the United States. If planted in a well-drained, sunny spot it will multiply vigorously and you will always have a supply. Choose well-developed, thick stems and cut close to the root with a sharp knife. The leaves are not used.

Stems of fresh lemon grass are becoming readily available at Asian food stores. The whole stem may be simmered in curries or soups and removed before serving. The only part used in pastes, or sliced finely in salads, is the tender white portion just above the root. Discard the outer layer, wash the lemon grass well and cut across into very thin slices using a sharp knife. This ensures there are no long fibres in the finished dishes.

If reduced to using strips of dried lemon grass, soak in hot water first. Or substitute 2 strips of thinly peeled lemon rind for each stem of lemon grass, peeling only the zest and leaving the bitter white pith behind.

Lily Buds

When you see a recipe using this ingredient, you may be sure it was originally Chinese. Slender golden buds are sold dried and should be soaked until soft. The flavour is very delicate and they may be omitted if they are difficult to find.

Lime

Thai: *Ma nao*
Bot: *Citrus aurantifolia*
Fam: *Rutaceae*

Small, deep green limes used for both rind and juice. Substitute any limes in season, or lemon.

Mung Beans, Split

A few years ago it was triumph indeed to find whole mung beans, ready to soak and sprout or to cook in various dishes. Now it is possible to purchase the split beans, skins removed, which makes it altogether more pleasant and practical to cook with them.

Mung Bean Flour

This white starch becomes clear when boiled with liquid and is used in the making of sweets. Substitute arrowroot or cornflour (cornstarch).

Noodles, Egg

Thai: *Ba mee*

Made from eggs and wheat flour, these noodles are the basis of many dishes, both stir-fried and in soups. They are used in dishes with a Burmese influence which are very popular in Northern Thailand.

Palm Sugar

Thai: *Nam tan peep*

Palm sugar comes from boiling down the sweet sap of coconut palms and palmyra palms. It can range from golden to dark brown, and while some of it is solid, in cakes, it is usually sold in jars and has the consistency of brown sugar mixed with treacle. Dark brown sugar makes a reasonable substitute if palm sugar proves elusive.

Pandanus or Screwpine

Thai: *Bai toey*
Bot: *Pandanus latifolia*
Fam: *Pandanaceae*

In Thai cooking the long, flat, fragrant green leaves are crushed and used as flavouring and colouring in sweets and sweet drinks or simmered with rice to impart their fragrance. The fresh leaves are also fashioned into tiny containers for sweets or wrapped around chicken before it is fried. The leaves are sold fresh, frozen or dried.

It is also possible to buy flavouring essence or paste made from pandanus leaves, the Asian equivalent of vanilla. This is most commonly labelled with its Malaysian name, *Pandan*, but I have also purchased it under its Thai name of *Bai toey*.

Peanut Oil

Peanut oil processed in the Western way has been refined and deodorised to the point where it has very little, if any, aroma and flavour. Oriental peanut oil, on the other hand, has a definite smell and taste of peanuts and is worth seeking out at Oriental stores. If it seems a bit strong to you at first, make a blend of half unrefined and half refined peanut oil, or whatever proportions suit your palate.

Pepper

Thai: *Prik thai*
Bot: *Piper nigrum*
Fam: *Piperaceae*

In Thailand, black pepper is one of the primary spices. In fact, though chillies are so entrenched in Thai food, it seems that pepper was used long before chillies were introduced around the 16th century. Green peppercorns are also used in Thai cooking, and may be tossed into dishes for extra flavour.

Pickled Garlic (*see* Garlic)

Rice

Thai: *Khao chao*

There are many varieties of rice. The kind most favoured as the mainstay of Thai meals is a white, long-grained rice with the faint scent of jasmine which occurs naturally. It should be cooked so it is tender and fluffy, without salt, because the seasonings and sauces in the accompanying dishes will provide all the saltiness required.

Glutinous or sticky rice (white) is mainly used in sweet snacks, but in some parts of Northern Thailand it is served with meals, as in neighbouring Laos. Black sticky rice, a special variety, is only served as a snack or sweet.

Rice Flour

Thai: *Pang khao chao*

Most Western supermarkets carry ground rice or rice flour in packets, and this is used to thicken sauces. Substitute cornflour (cornstarch) if necessary. Glutinous rice flour, *pang khao niew*, is used in certain desserts.

Roasted Rice Flour (*see* Rice, Roasted and Ground)

Rice Noodles

Thai: *Kway teo*

These white noodles come in many sizes, and while some are so fine they need only a minute or two in boiling water, others which are thicker should first be soaked, then cooked until tender. A great variety of dried rice noodles may be purchased at all Asian supermarkets. In Thailand, the rice noodles are made freshly each morning and may be sold in strands, or in large squares for the cook to cut.

Rice Vermicelli

Thai: *Sen mee*

The finest variety of rice noodles, these are usually ready to serve after soaking in boiling water. They may also be dropped straight into boiling water for a minute, or into boiling oil for a few seconds, as for *Mee Grob* (*page 149*). They increase in size dramatically, so fry only a small handful at a time and remove from the oil to drain on absorbent paper. The *mee* should puff and swell within seconds, otherwise it means the oil is not hot enough.

Rice, Roasted and Ground

At one time I used to roast and grind the rice myself, but now it is possible to buy small packets of ready-roasted rice flour. It is considered an essential part of some recipes in which it is sprinkled over a savoury dish, but to the untrained palate it is not detectable. If it proves too much of a hassle it may be omitted.

Sago

Thai: *Sa-ku*

The starch obtained from the sago palm and other plants with a starchy pith. It looks like little white pearls which when cooked should become clear with no white centre. This is used in both savoury and sweet dishes.

Sesame Seeds

Thai: *Nga*
Bot: *Sesamum indicum*
Fam: *Pedaliaceae*

In Thai cooking, these nutritious seeds are used mainly for flavouring sweets (usually lightly roasted and ground). White sesame seeds are preferable to black sesame or unhulled seeds. Available at Asian markets and health food stores.

Shallots

Thai: *Hom lek*
Bot: *Allium ascalonicum*
Fam: *Liliaceae, Alliaceae, Amaryllidaceae*

Shallots are small, golden brown, purplish or grey bulbs growing in clusters like garlic. They are not slender white bulbs with green tops though, especially in Australia, this is a common mistake. (These are spring onions or scallions.) Shallots are an important ingredient in Thai cooking, but because they are sometimes hard to find, white or brown onions or spring onions may be substituted.

When crisp fried shallots or onions are needed for a recipe, buy them already fried in a packet or tub and save yourself a deal of time and trouble. Store in the freezer to keep from going rancid. If you do not have access to Oriental grocery stores, substitute dried onions which can be fried in a little oil, removed as soon as they turn slightly deeper coloured, and drained on absorbent paper.

Shiitake Mushrooms

Thai: *Hed hom*

Bot: *Lentinus edodes*

Because they are dried and imported, these fragrant mushrooms are not cheap but they do add a quite distinctive flavour to Chinese-influenced Thai dishes. Do not substitute dried Continental mushrooms, as the flavour is quite different.

Shrimp, Dried

Thai: *Goong haeng*

These are sold in plastic packets. A good way to judge the quality is by the colour, which should be salmon pink, and by pressing the shrimps through the packet – they should be slightly yielding, not hard like chips of wood. Above all, they should not smell strongly of ammonia. Keep the packets refrigerated. If ever they develop a strong or unpleasant smell after long storage, rinse them well in warm water and leave to dry. They will keep for quite a long time but if they start to disintegrate and become powdery, throw them out.

Shrimp Paste

Thai: *Kapi*

Small shrimps are salted and dried in the sun, the liquid which they give off is bottled and matured to make *nam pla*, and the residue goes to make shrimp paste. Pungent enough to warrant being enclosed in a screw-topped bottle, it needs no refrigeration. Use Chinese shrimp sauce or Malaysian *blacan*, or anchovy paste as a substitute.

Spring Onions (Scallions)

Thai: *Ton hom*
Bot: *Allium cepa or Allium fistulosum*
Fam: *Liliaceae*

Spring onions are the thinnings of either *Allium cepa* or *A. fistulum* plantings that do not form a bulb. Strangely, in Australia these are commonly known as shallots.

Straw Mushrooms

Thai: *Hed farng*
Bot: *Volvariella volvaceae*

This cultivated mushroom consists of a sheath within which is the mushroom. The sheath is edible too. If bought fresh the mushrooms should be blanched in boiling water for a few minutes. They are also available canned or dried. Substitute button mushrooms or champignons.

Sweet Red Ginger

Purchased in bottles, slices of ginger are preserved in sugar syrup, both syrup and ginger being coloured red. This makes a nice addition to a sauce for fish.

Tamarind

Thai: *Ma kham*
Bot: *Tamarindus indica*
Fam: *Leguminoseae*

Tamarind is a tropical tree which bears large, long beans with brittle brown shells containing large, hard seeds. The seeds are surrounded by a sweetish-sour brown pulp, which gives a distinctive acid flavour quite different to lemon juice or vinegar.

Tamarind may be purchased in various forms. It may be dried together with the seeds and fibres, only the shell being removed. Or it may be dried without the seeds.

If using **dried tamarind**, take a piece the size of a walnut and soak in ½ cup (4 fl oz) of hot water for 10 minutes. Knead and rub with your fingers until the pulp dissolves in the water, and then strain out the seeds and fibres. This is what I refer to as **tamarind liquid**.

One may also purchase **tamarind pulp**. The one I like to use is about as thick as plum sauce – a heavy pouring consistency. Two tablespoons of this tamarind pulp concentrate is equal to 1 rounded tablespoon of the dried tamarind which has been soaked in ½ cup (4 fl oz) hot water and then strained.

There is another form of **instant tamarind** which is so hard that it seems to take longer to dissolve it in water than it does to soak and strain the tamarind pulp. Whichever form you use, taste it for acidity and use a little at first, adding more if necessary for a piquant flavour.

Tapioca Flour

Thai: *Pang mun*

A clear starch for making sweets

Tempeh

A fermented cake made from soy beans, this features as the 'new health food' and supplies first class protein in vegetarian meals. Firmer and more flavourful than tofu or bean curd, it is worth investigating.

Turmeric

Thai: *Kha-min*
Bot: *Curcuma longa*
Fam: *Zingiberaceae*

A bright yellow rhizome from which the familiar yellow powder, mainstay of cheap curry powders, is obtained. In Thailand most turmeric is used fresh.

Water Chestnut

Thai: *Haeo*
Bot: *Eleocharis tuberosa*

Crisp, slightly sweet, off-white within a dark brownish-black skin which must be peeled off, the so-called chestnut is not a nut at all, but the tuber of a sedge. It is used in savoury as well as sweet dishes and is prized for its crisp texture which is retained even through cooking. More readily available canned than fresh.

Wood Fungus (*see* Black Fungus)

White Glutinous Rice (*see* Rice)

Notes on pronunciation of Thai words

You don't have to speak Thai to enjoy the flavours of Thailand, but it helps if one can recognise famous dishes when they are called only by their Thai names. Some are so well known that even *farang* (foreigners) would not dream of ordering anything other than *Mee Grob* or *Tom Yum Goong*. But if you expect even the simplest name to be spelled the same way on every menu, you will surely be disappointed.

The letters K and G seem to be interchangeable, so are L and R. *Kaeng* or *gaeng* are the same, and rhyme with *gang* – sort of. Chicken is *gai* or *kai* (rhymes with 'sky'), but I am told that *kai* also means 'egg'. So, arbitrarily perhaps, I have used *gai* for chicken, *kai* for egg.

Prawns are *kung* or *goong*, but the vowel(s) are like the 'u' in 'put', even if to the Anglo-Saxon eye it seems reasonable that *kung* should rhyme with *hung*. Thus, *Lug Chup* ('look choop') testifies to the validity of that rule, but in a *yum* (salad), it is 'u' as in 'hut'. We didn't use *yam* because there would be the temptation to pronounce it like a sweet potato!

To prevent similar understandable errors, my Thai friend, Rachnee (Dang) Howarth, spent hours translating recipe titles, with phonetic spelling so they could be pronounced correctly by enthusiasts who cannot speak Thai. I am immensely grateful to her.

Here are the ground rules.

A as in 'father' or the 'u' sound in 'but'
AE rhymes with 'gang', but more drawn out
AI rhymes with 'why'
AO rhymes with 'cow'
E as in 'pet'
I as in 'pit'
O as in 'or'
U most often as in 'put', sometimes as in 'putt'.

G as in 'goat'
J as in 'joke'
CH as in 'chew'
PH as in 'pet'. (The two letters do not combine to give the 'f' sound.)

Recipe Index

Rose petal salad	*yum dok gulab*	75
Lobster and mandarin salad	*yum goong gub som*	75
Crab salad	*pla-poo*	77
Crab and water chestnut salad	*yum poo gub haeo-chin*	77
Beef salad	*yum nuer*	78
Cucumber cactus flower		79
Dried shrimp salad with lemon grass	*yum goong haeng*	79
Fresh salad with nam prik	*pak nam prik*	80
Grilled eggplant and dried shrimp salad	*yum makua pao*	82
Nam prik Phuket		82
Shrimp dip with tamarind	*nam prik pao*	84
Pork and peanut dip	*moo lon*	84
Sweet chilli sauce	*saus prik wan*	84
Sweet dipping sauce	*saus wan*	85
Eggplant dipping sauce	*nam prik makua*	85
Chilli sauce	*saus prik*	85

Fish and Other Seafood

Whole fried fish with mushroom & ginger sauce	*platod lard khing hedhom*	88
Giant stuffed prawns	*goong sod sai*	88
Green curry of prawns	*kaeng khiew wan goong*	89
Stuffed fried crab	*poo cha*	90
Fish ball curry with vegetables	*kaeng phed look chin pla, pak*	90
Stuffed curried mussels	*hor mok mang poo*	92
Hot and sour prawns with cucumbers	*goong lon tang-gwa*	94
Steamed fish with tamarind and ginger	*planung khing*	94
Fried fish with tamarind sauce	*pla jian*	95
Red curry of prawns	*kaeng phed goong*	96
Fried prawn balls	*look chin goong tod*	96
Curry of crab claws and prawn balls	*kaeng phed gampoo, look chin goong*	98
Crab claws with chilli sauce	*gampoo yudsai lard prik*	98
Chilli prawn with shredded lime leaf	*phat prik goong bai makrut*	100
Pomfret with coconut	*pla lard kati*	100
Red curry of crab	*kaeng phed poo*	101

Poultry

Roast duck curry with pineapple	*kaeng phed ped yang subparot*	105
Chicken in spicy peanut sauce	*gai phad saus tua*	105
Barbecued garlic chicken	*gai yang*	106
Chicken curry	*kaeng gai*	106
Chicken fillet with snow peas	*kaeng khiew wan gai tua*	108
Chicken and sataw nuts	*gai phad sataw*	108
Stuffed chicken wings	*peek gai yud sai*	111
Peanut sauce	*nam jim tua*	111
Duck with lychees	*kaeng ped linjee*	112
Grilled spiced quail	*nok-krata yang*	114
Chicken and vegetables with chilli-shrimp sauce	*gai pak phad nam prik*	114
Chilli chicken with noodles	*kway teo phad*	115
Chicken with ginger and wood fungus	*gai phad khing hed hung*	116
Chiang Mai chicken salad	*larb gai Chiang Mai*	118
Son-in-law eggs	*kai look koei*	118
Chicken with beans	*gai phad tua*	119
Chicken and bamboo shoot curry	*kaeng phed gai nor mai*	119
Chicken salad with vegetables	*yum tha wai*	120
Chicken and vegetable soup	*kaeng chud gai pak*	122
Fried chicken with basil	*phad gai bai kraprao*	122
Chicken and straw mushroom curry	*phad phed gai hed farng*	123
Duck Masaman curry	*Masaman ped*	123

Meat

Masaman beef curry	*kaeng Masaman nuer*	126
Sweet pork	*moo wan*	126
Red pork curry with young corn	*kaeng phed moo kao poad orn*	128

Spicy pork mince	*phad moo sub*	*128*
Stir-fried chilli pork with cashews	*moo phad mamuang mimaparn*	*131*
Mixed satay		*131*
Minced beef salad	*larb*	*132*
Beef Panang curry	*Panang nuer*	*132*
Green curry of beef	*kaeng khiew wan nuer*	*133*
Beef and spinach in coconut milk	*kaeng nuer gub pak kom*	*133*
Minced beef with dried shrimp	*phad nuer sub goong haeng*	*133*
Pork and crab sausage	*sai klok moo gub poo*	*134*
Fried meat balls	*moo, nuer tod mun*	*136*
Sweet and hot crisp beef	*nuer khem phad*	*136*
Pork curry with ginger and pickled garlic	*moo phad khing kratiem dong*	*137*
Eggs filled with pork and seafood	*eggs filled with por- Thai name*	*137*
Pork with bitter gourd	*khiew wan mara yud sai moo*	*139*
Pork Panang curry	*Panang moo*	*139*
Beef and pumpkin curry	*kaeng nuer fug tong*	*141*
Stir-fried beef with broccoli and corn	*phad phed nuer, kao poad orn*	*141*
Minced pork with basil	*moo sub bai kraprao*	*141*
Fried beef with bamboo shoot & mushrooms	*phad nuer normai, hed*	*142*

Rice and Noodles

Rice: steamer method		*148*
Rice: absorption method		*148*
Crab fried rice in omelette	*kai yud sai khao poo*	*148*
Rice: glutinous	*Khao niew*	*149*
Deep-fried crispy rice noodles	*mee grob*	*149*
Iced rice	*khao chae*	*150*
Cold bean thread salad	*yum woon sen*	*150*
Rice and coconut pancakes	*khanom krok*	*152*
Rice noodles with chicken and prawns	*kway teo phat gai goong*	*152*
Deep-fried rice crackers with dips	*khao tang-na tang*	*154*
Bean starch noodles with chicken	*kai phad woon sen*	*154*
Floating market soup noodles	*kway teo ruer*	*156*
Fried egg noodles with barbecued pork	*ba mee phat moo yang*	*159*
Rice noodles with hot seasonings	*sen mee phat nuer*	*159*
Whole Earth vegetarian noodles	*phat mee jeh*	*161*
Mixed fried rice	*khao phat ruam mit*	*162*
Pork balls with noodles	*ba mee look chin moo*	*162*

Vegetables

Cabbage with prawns and pork loin	*moo goong, kalum plee*	*166*
Filled and fried eggplant	*makua sod sai tod*	*166*
Fried bean curd in coconut milk	*tao hu tom kha*	*168*
Stir-fried water chestnuts and snow peas	*pad haeo chine, tua lun tao*	*169*
Water convolvulus with dried shrimp	*pak boong phad goong haeng*	*169*
Fried bean curd and mixed vegetables	*tao hu phad pak pason*	*169*
Stir-fried eggplant with tempeh	*makua phad tempeh*	*170*
Stir-fried asparagus	*phad nor mai farang*	*170*
Stir-fried spinach	*phad pak kom*	*170*
Bean curd in cabbage rolls	*kalum plee pan tao hu*	*172*
Eggplant with bean curd	*phad ma kua tao hu*	*172*
Banana capsicum curry	*kaeng prik yuak sod sai*	*175*
Tempeh curry	*lon tempeh*	*175*
Eggplant in batter	*makua chup pang tod*	*175*
Cauliflower with Thai spinach	*pad pak kom, dom galum*	*176*
Stuffed zucchini	*sod sai zucchini*	*176*
Ridged gourd curry	*gaeng khiew wan buab liam*	*178*
Mixed vegetables in coconut milk	*tom kati pak ruam*	*178*

Thai Desserts and Sweet Snacks

Mangoes with sweet rice	*khao niew ma muang*	*182*
Bananas in sago cream	*gluay saku kati*	*182*

General Index
Numerals in bold type indicate a photograph